WRITE CUT REWRITE

It was on a dreary night of November that I beheld ~~the frame on whic~~ ~~my~~ man compleated; ~~and~~ with an anxiety that almost amounted to agony I collected instruments of life around me ~~and endeavoured to~~ that I might infuse a spark of being into the lifeless thing that lay at my feet. It was already one in the morning, the rain pattered dismally against the window panes, & my candle was nearly burnt out, when by the glimmer of the half extinguished light I saw the dull yellow eye of the creature open — It breathed hard, and a convulsive motion agitated its limbs.

~~But how~~ How can I describe my emotion at this catastrophe; or how delineate the wretch whom with such infinite pains and care I had endeavoured to form. His limbs were in proportion and I had selected his features ~~&~~ as ~~handsome handsome~~. beautiful. ~~Handsome~~ Beautiful; Great God! His yellow ~~skin~~ skin scarcely covered the work of

WRITE CUT REWRITE

THE CUTTING-ROOM FLOOR OF MODERN LITERATURE

Dirk Van Hulle & Mark Nixon

BODLEIAN
LIBRARY
PUBLISHING

This publication has been generously supported by the Martin J. Gross Family Foundation

This work was supported by the Arts and Humanities Research Council [grant number AH/W002663/1]

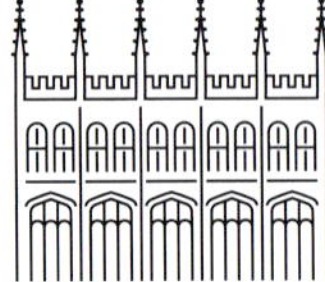

First published in 2024 by Bodleian Library Publishing
Broad Street, Oxford OX1 3BG

www.bodleianshop.co.uk

ISBN 978 1 85124 618 2

Publisher: Samuel Fanous
Managing Editor: Susie Foster
Editor: Janet Phillips
Picture Editor: Leanda Shrimpton
Cover design by Dot Little at the Bodleian Library
Designed and typeset by Lucy Morton of illuminati in 10.8 on 16 Minion
Printed and bound by Printer Trento S.r.l. on 150gsm Gardamatt Art paper

British Library Catalogue in Publishing Data
A CIP record of this publication is available from the British Library

CONTENTS

FOREWORD

As one of the oldest libraries in Europe, the Bodleian is world famous for its long-standing manuscript collections. Many of these collections contain medieval treasures, written by scribes in the most beautiful hands and adorned with picture-postcard illuminations. But the library also holds numerous manuscripts produced in more recent times, not made by professional scribes but written in the sometimes near-illegible hand of the author, full of deletions, additions, notes and scribbles.

These drafts, containing fragments that were never published, are often discarded; studying this type of material has sometimes been regarded as akin to rummaging in writers' waste-paper baskets. But it is of course precisely because writers have chosen *not* to throw it away that this material ended up in libraries and archives in the first place. They were aware that their published texts could not have taken shape without the parts that had to be cut.

Michelangelo is believed to have said that the sculpture was already complete within the marble block before he started his work; he just had to chisel away the superfluous material. He made it seem as if he simply needed to extract what was already there. The 'cuts' that he made were just as essential as what was left untouched for the statue to emerge.

How crucial the act of cutting can be is especially clear in the film industry. The director's cut is seldom the final cut meant for the film's public release. Evidently, that does not necessarily mean that the director's cut is of inferior quality. On the contrary, it is often very revealing to see what the director's view on the movie was and which compromises had to be made in the last phases of production.

In literature, the act of cutting is equally crucial. Alongside the 2024 exhibition *Write Cut Rewrite* at the Bodleian Library, curated by Dirk Van Hulle and Mark Nixon, this book emphasizes the central role of 'killing your darlings' in creative writing. It unearths numerous notes, drafts and snippets that seldom see the light of day. They were edited or expurgated for various reasons, sometimes against the author's will, as an act of censorship.

Since these cuts did not make it into the published text, archives and libraries like the Bodleian are often the only places where they can be explored. They are the 'what if's of literature. To take a famous example, would T.S. Eliot's *The Waste Land* have had the same impact if Ezra Pound had not pruned and reduced it to half of its original length? What if Edgar Allan Poe had decided not to replace his initial idea for the bird that keeps saying 'Nevermore', and his famous poem *The Raven* had been called *The Parrot*? Or, to take some specific examples from this book, what would *Frankenstein* have looked like if Mary and Percy Shelley had not collaborated on the draft? Would we view *The Wind in the Willows* differently if its title had remained 'The Mole & the Water Rat'? The following chapters invite you to explore these roads-not-taken and discover the most intriguing vistas. The Bodleian would like to express our great thanks to Dirk Van Hulle and Mark Nixon for showing us the way.

Richard Ovenden OBE
Bodley's Librarian

rate – of one or two things which Style is not; which have little or nothing to do with Style, though sometimes vulgarly mistaken for it. Style, for example, is not – can never be – extraneous ornament. You remember, may be, the Persian lover whom I quoted to you out of Newman; how to convey his passion he sought a professional letter-writer who, duly instructed, forthwith dipped the pen of desire in the ink of devotedness and proceeded to spread it over the page of desolation; whereupon the nightingale of affection was heard to warble to the rose of loveliness, while the breeze of anxiety played around the brow of expectation. Here, in this extraneous, professional, purchased ornamentation, you have something which Style is not : and if you require a practical rule of me, I will present you with this.– 'Whenever, being under the age of fifty (beyond which term experience has scarcely carried me) you feel an impulse to perpetrate a piece of exceptionally fine writing, obey it – obey it whole-heartedly – and tear it up before sending your manuscript to press. Murder your darlings.'

– I never promised you that a writer's was an easy life.

But let me plead further that you have not been left altogether without clue to the secret of what Style is. That you must follow the clue & master the secret for yourselves lay implicit in our bargain, & (I repeat) you were never promised that a writer's life would be easy. Yet a clue was certainly put in your hands when having insisted that Literature is a living Art, I added that therefore it must be personal and of its essence personal.

This goes very deep: it conditions all our criticism of art, – and of literature which is an art; yet it conceals no mystery. You may see its mean

INTRODUCTION
'KILL YOUR DARLINGS'

Imagine yourself, sitting at your computer, writing an email in reply to a message that made you quite angry. Your first impulse is to write a strong message that conveys your extreme displeasure. You almost press the send button. But you have been taught to avoid sending angry emails, and so you let it rest for a few hours and start rewriting it. Writing almost always involves cutting and rewriting. This applies to everyday practices such as writing an email or a text message, and even more so to writing poetry or fiction. As one of the most successful fiction authors ever, Stephen King gives the following advice: 'that's what most of us end up having to do (kill your darlings, kill your darlings, even when it breaks your egocentric little scribbler's heart, kill your darlings)'.[1] The phrase 'kill your darlings' is often attributed to the American modernist author William Faulkner, but he borrowed it from the British author Sir Arthur Quiller-Couch (1863–1944). On Wednesday, 28 January 1914, Quiller-Couch delivered a lecture at the University of Cambridge entitled 'On Style' – as part of a lecture series 'On the Art of Writing' – and gave the audience this 'practical rule':

> Whenever ... you feel an impulse to perpetrate a piece of exceptionally fine writing, obey it – obey it whole-heartedly – and tear it up before sending your manuscript to press. *Murder your darlings.*[2] (SEE FIG. 32)

He practised what he preached and even cut his own surname, writing under the pseudonym Q. Obviously, the metaphor of 'killing' or 'murdering' is chosen for dramatic effect. Usually, cutting, cancelling or otherwise undoing what you have written is so common that we hardly notice it. But in literature that means numerous passages have been undone by writers and never made it to publication. These cuts are the focal point of this book.

The act of deleting is a crucial component of the creative process in modern literature. And yet we seldom get to see any traces of this process, partly because writers often make cuts in the privacy of their drafts. And if they do not wish anyone to see these private documents, they burn or shred them. But there are also many writers who keep their manuscripts. After all, writing is often a laborious process. A volume of poetry is not just a work of literature, but also the work that goes into it. It is both a product and a process. And manuscripts testify to the work it takes to produce a poem, a play, an essay or a novel.

As material 'things', manuscripts have 'agency'. To illustrate the agency of things, Bruno Latour gives the example of a gun:

> You are different with a gun in your hand; the gun is different with you holding it. You are another subject because you hold the gun; the gun is another object because it has entered into a relationship with you. The gun is no longer the gun-in-the-armoury or the gun-in-the-drawer or the gun-in-the-pocket, but the gun-in-your-hand, aimed at someone who is screaming.[3]

The agency of manuscripts may not be so dramatic, but it exists. It is not so theatrical, because manuscripts are usually kept behind the scenes. Latour's 'actor network theory' has done a lot to puncture the false dichotomy between active persons and passive objects, and so has Bill Brown's 'thing theory'. Their great merit is that they let objects assert themselves as things, instead of looking through them. Whoever makes this point about the agency of things, however, tends to take their *presence* for granted. But, as Severin Fowles notes, sometimes it is not so much the presence but the absence of something that has agency.[4] Suppose you are in a crowded Underground train, and you suddenly feel your smartphone is no longer in your pocket. Then it is the *absence* of your phone that has a shock effect. It is an absence that is felt. It is real. It is 'present', so to speak.

This type of present absence is central to this book. Libraries such as the Bodleian keep hundreds of things that have been cut and therefore never made it into a book publication. They are absent in literature. You do not notice them, but if you know about them their cutting can sometimes feel like an almost palpable absence (or presence). When you know that Jane Austen's novel *Persuasion* originally had a different ending; when you know that for a description in *Frankenstein* Mary Shelley cut an entry from Percy Shelley's journal; when you know that *The Wind in the Willows* initially had a different title; when you know that the censor cut several passages from Samuel Beckett's *Waiting for Godot*, these cuts become present absences, and they can suddenly feel like the absence of your smartphone in the crowded Underground.

freedom of his manner

by a gracious answer, & a more full view of her face than she had yet bestowed. Unused to exert himself, & happy in contemplating her, he sat in silence for some minutes longer, while Tom Musgrave was chattering to Elizth, till they were interrupted by Nanny's half ... the door & putting

1

AUTHORS' CUTS

ORMVLVM

THIS BOOK FOCUSES on 'modern' manuscripts. In this context, the term 'modern' is used to distinguish these documents from older – for instance, medieval – manuscripts, most of which are not in the author's own hand. The majority of medieval manuscripts were made by scribes, who copied them to share them with a wider community, and so their function was a form of distribution. Modern manuscripts, however, are usually in the author's own hand and their function is typically not distribution. On the contrary, they are usually private documents. Before the early modern period, most autograph manuscripts were generally discarded once they were copied. The middle of the eighteenth century is often taken as the starting point of the 'modern' manuscript. That does not mean there are no autograph private manuscripts from earlier periods (especially in literatures such as the Italian tradition), but in literature in English these are quite rare. An example of such a manuscript is the so-called *Ormulum*, a twelfth-century series of homilies or commentaries on the Bible by a man called Orm (SEE FIG. 1). It is written on pieces of parchment of the lowest quality: the edges of hides.

As a result, the pages are often not rectangular but have irregular shapes. For a notebook that is almost a thousand years old it looks surprisingly modern because it features so many crossed-out passages. It really shows someone in mid-thought, using a quill and parchment to give shape to their ideas. But this example is so rare that it can be seen as an exception confirming the rule that the majority of early manuscripts in English are by scribes, not by the authors themselves. Most of the examples in this book are therefore no older than the eighteenth century.

1 The *Ormulum*, a twelfth-century manuscript of commentaries on the Bible, identified as the earliest surviving autograph manuscript in English (written by Orm) (Oxford, Bodleian Library, MS. Junius 1, fols 7v–10r)

† Let such teach others who themselves excell,
And censure freely who have written well.
Authors are partial to their Wit, 'tis true,
But are not Criticks to their Judgment too?

yet if we look more closely, we shall find
* Most have the Seeds of Judgment in their Mind;
Nature affords at least a glimm'ring Light;
The Lines, tho' ~~touch'd~~ touch'd but faintly, are drawn right.
But as the Slightest Sketch, if justly trac'd,
Is by ill Colouring but the more disgrac'd,
(25) So by false Learning is good Sense defac'd;
~~(Good Sense, which only is the Gift of Heav'n,~~
~~And tho no Science, yet is worth the Sev'n.)~~
~~Many are spoil'd by that Pedantic Throng,~~
~~Who, with great Pains, teach youth to reason wrong.~~
~~Tutors like Virtuoso's, oft, inclin'd~~
~~By strange Transfusion to improve the Mind,~~
~~Draw off the Sense we have, to pour in new;~~
~~Which yet, with all their Skill, they ne'r could do.~~
~~Thus some are wilder'd~~ Some are bewilder'd in the Maze of Schools,
And some made Coxcombs Nature meant ~~but~~ Fools.
(without a break) — In search of Wit ~~some~~ these lose their common Sense,
And then turn Criticks in their own Defence.
~~Some~~ Those hate as Rivals all that write; and others
But envy Wits, as Eunuchs envy Lovers.
All Fools have still an Itching to deride,
And fain would be upon the Laughing Side:
~~Tho' such with reason Men of Sense abhor,~~
~~Fool against Fool is barb'rous Civil War;~~
~~St~~ Tho' Mævius scribble, and the City Knight, (34)
There are, who judge still worse than they can write.

(left margin: ~~Cancel these~~ Transcribe all these) — or Pedants [illegible] — Good Sense [illegible] do.)
(left margin: ~~a Prudence [illegible]~~ ~~or [illegible]~~)
(left margin: del Transcribe)
(right margin: 3d page)

Some

† Qui scribit artificiosè, ab aliis commodè scripta facile intelligere poterit. Cic. ad Herenn. lib. 4.
—De Pictore, Sculptore, Fictore, nisi Artifex judicare non potest. Pliny.

* Omnes tacito quodam sensu, sine ulla arte, aut ratione, quæ sint in artibus ac rationibus recta ac prava dijudicant. Cic. de Orat. lib. 3.
—~~Plus sine Doctrina Prudentia quam sine prudentia valet Doctrina.~~ Quintil.
—~~Adolescentulos existimo in Scholis stultissimos fieri, qui nil ex his quæ in usu habemus, aut audiant, aut vident.~~ Petronius.

The gen'rous Critick fann'd the Poet's Fire,
And taught the World, with Reason to Admire.
Then Criticisme the Muses Handmaid prov'd,
To dress her Charms and make her more belov'd;
But following Wits from that Intention stray'd;
Who cou'd not win the Mistress, woo'd the Maid,
Set up themselves, and drove a sep'rate Trade: }
B. pbr. 9 [Against the Poets their own Arms they turn'd,
Sure to hate most the Men from whom they learn'd.
So modern Pothecaries, taught the Art
By Doctor's Bills to play the Doctor's Part,
Bold in the practise of mistaken Rules,
Prescribe, apply, and call their Masters Fools.
Some on the Leaves of ancient Authors prey,
Nor Time nor Moths e'er spoil'd so much as they:
Some dryly plain, without Invention's Aid,
Write dull Receits how Poems may be made:
* These lost the Sense, their Learning to display;
And those explain'd the Meaning quite away.

You then whose Judgment the right Course wou'd steer,
Know well each Ancient's proper Character,
His Fable, Subject, Scope in ev'ry Page,
Religion, Country, Genius of his Age:
Without all these at once before your Eyes,
You may Confound, but never Criticize.
~~Zoilus had these been known, without a Name~~ from Page (24. to. 25.)
~~Had dy'd, and Perault ne'r been damn'd to Fame~~; Transcribe these.
dele The Sense of sound Antiquity had reign'd,
And Sacred Homer yet been unprophan'd.
None e'er had thought His Comprehensive Mind
To modern Customs, modern Rules confin'd,
Who for All Ages writ, and All Mankind! }

Be

Deletions and substitutions

Alexander Pope, for instance, prepared a manuscript of *An Essay on Criticism* which contains many famous lines, such as 'To err is human; to forgive, divine' and 'Fools rush in where angels fear to tread'. The manuscript also features several deletions, such as the passage on pedantic teachers: 'Many are spoil'd by that Pedantic Throng / Who, with great Pains, teach Youth to reason wrong' (SEE FIG. 2).[5] These lines are part of an eight-line passage that was crossed out by Pope before the *Essay* was first published in 1711. As Robert M. Schmitz notes, the 'manuscript of 804 lines was trimmed down to a printed text of 745'.[6]

Soon after the first edition, other editions appeared with footnotes indicating that Pope had made several cuts. For instance, in the 1751 edition by 'Mr. Warburton' of *The Works of Alexander Pope Esq. in Nine Volumes Complete*, a footnote quotes these cuts with the following explanation: 'Between v[erse] 25 and 26 were these lines, since omitted by the author'.[7] The manuscript has a title page that mimics a printed title page, suggesting that it was probably meant to serve as a printer's copy. Pope specified to the printer as precisely as possible what he wanted his title page to look like. But this precision with respect to layout did not prevent him from making changes to the text. He kept revising, which meant above all: cutting.

In the beginning of the eighteenth century, the so-called 'battle of the books' was raging, the quarrel of the 'Ancients' and the 'Moderns'. Like Swift, Pope was on the side of the Ancients. He believed that to become a good writer it was imperative that you study the examples of the Ancient Greek and Roman authors. His advice in *An Essay on Criticism* is:

Be *Homer*'s Works your *Study* and *Delight*,
Read them by Day, and meditate by Night,
Thence from your Judgment, thence your Notions bring,
And trace the *Muses upward* to their *Spring*.

In the manuscript, Pope cut the preceding seven lines (SEE FIG. 3). According to him, it was necessary to 'Know well each Ancient's proper Character', their religion, their country, the 'Genius of his Age': you cannot criticize 'Without all these at once before your Eyes'. If people would apply these rules, writers like Perrault would never have been 'damn'd to Fame':

PRECEDING PAGES

2 Manuscript of Alexander Pope's *Essay on Criticism* with deleted passages, such as 'Many are spoil'd by that Pedantic Throng / Who, with great Pains, teach Youth to reason wrong' (Oxford, Bodleian Library, MS. Eng. poet. C. 1, fol. 2v)

3 Manuscript of Alexander Pope's *Essay on Criticism* with the phrase 'damn'd to Fame' (six lines from the bottom) deleted (Oxford, Bodleian Library, MS. Eng. poet. C. 1, fol. 4r)

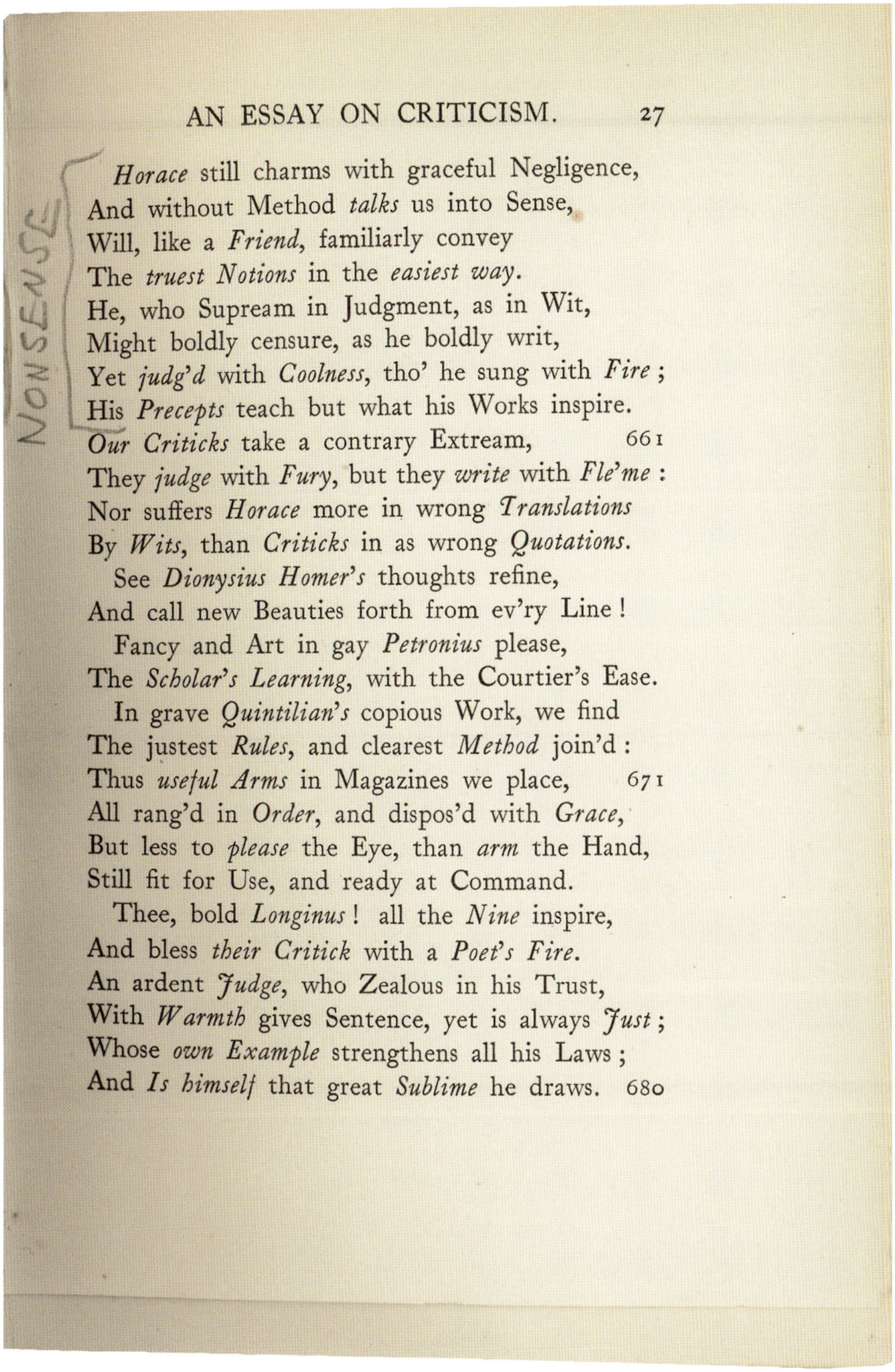

AN ESSAY ON CRITICISM. 27

Horace still charms with graceful Negligence,
And without Method *talks* us into Sense,
Will, like a *Friend*, familiarly convey
The *truest Notions* in the *easiest way.*
He, who Supream in Judgment, as in Wit,
Might boldly censure, as he boldly writ,
Yet *judg'd* with *Coolness*, tho' he sung with *Fire* ;
His *Precepts* teach but what his Works inspire.
Our Criticks take a contrary Extream,
They *judge* with *Fury*, but they *write* with *Fle'me* :
Nor suffers *Horace* more in wrong *Translations*
By *Wits*, than *Criticks* in as wrong *Quotations.*
See *Dionysius Homer's* thoughts refine,
And call new Beauties forth from ev'ry Line !
Fancy and Art in gay *Petronius* please,
The *Scholar's Learning*, with the Courtier's Ease.
In grave *Quintilian's* copious Work, we find
The justest *Rules*, and clearest *Method* join'd :
Thus *useful Arms* in Magazines we place,
All rang'd in *Order*, and dispos'd with *Grace*,
But less to *please* the Eye, than *arm* the Hand,
Still fit for Use, and ready at Command.
Thee, bold *Longinus* ! all the *Nine* inspire,
And bless *their Critick* with a *Poet's Fire.*
An ardent *Judge*, who Zealous in his Trust,
With *Warmth* gives Sentence, yet is always *Just* ;
Whose *own Example* strengthens all his Laws ;
And *Is himself* that great *Sublime* he draws.

4 Samuel Beckett's annotated copy of Pope's *Essay on Criticism* (Beckett Digital Library, www.beckettarchive.org/library/POP-ESS.html)

Zoilus, had these been known, without a Name
Had dy'd, and Perrault ne'r been damn'd to Fame;
The Sense of sound Antiquity had reign'd;
And Sacred Homer yet been unprophan'd.
None e'er had thought His Comprehensive Mind
To modern Customs, modern Rules confin'd,
Who for All Ages writ, and All Mankind![8]

This whole passage was crossed out and Pope wrote 'dele' next to it in the left margin, the Latin equivalent of the imperative 'cut' or 'delete'. In the following lines, on the next page, Pope is still tinkering with the phrasing of this passage. Initially he wrote: 'Be ~~his great~~ Works your Study and Delight'. He considered replacing 'Be' by 'Make', but then deleted '~~Make~~' again, and he replaced '~~his great~~ Works' by 'Homer's Works' (fol. 3v). Homer needed to be mentioned by name since, the preceding seven lines having been cut, it was no longer clear what 'his' referred to.

The expression 'damn'd to fame' may have been cut, but it was not entirely lost, for Pope recycled it later in *The Dunciad*. That is where Samuel Beckett found it. He jotted it down in one of his notebooks,[9] and that – in turn – is where James Knowlson found it as the source of inspiration for the title of his biography, *Damned to Fame: The Life of Samuel Beckett* (1996).[10] Beckett had a copy of *The Poetical Works of Alexander Pope* (Gall & Inglis, Edinburgh, 1881[?]) among the books in his extant library, as well as *An Essay on Criticism* (ed. John Sergeant, Clarendon Press, Oxford, 1909), in which he marked a few passages, notably one about Horace. When Pope waxes lyrical about the way Horace sung with fire but judged with coolness, conveying the truest notions in the easiest way, Beckett pencilled in the left margin in capital letters: 'NONSENSE' (SEE FIG. 4).[11]

Beckett, in his turn, was very critical of his own writings, as the mere shape of some of his cancellations in his manuscripts shows (SEE FIG. 5). The first draft of the play *Not I*, for instance, opens with the birth of a baby. This version is first cancelled by means of a big St Andrew's cross, and then, in a second phase, crossed out even more energetically with a thick black felt-tip marker. Beckett drew a line underneath that first draft and, on the very same page, he started a second draft, in which 'tiny ~~baby~~' was deleted and became 'tiny little thing'. The act of cancelling was not necessarily a manner of omitting, but a way of forcing himself to revise and rewrite, according to Louise Bourgeois' principle 'I do, I undo and I redo.'[12]

5 Samuel Beckett, manuscript of the play *Not I* (University of Reading, UoR MS 1227/7/12/1, fol. 1r)

PARIS
20.3.72

I

As house lights down voice unintelligible behind curtain. House lights out. Voice continues unintelligible behind curtain. 10 seconds. As curtain rises ... birth into this world ... ad lib ... [illegible] place ... leading when [illegible] fully up

Stage in darkness but for MOUTH, upstage audience R, convenient level, faintly lit from close up & below, as little as possible of rest of face, invisible microphone. AUDITOR, downstage audience L, tall upright figure enveloped from head to foot in black djellaba, shown by attitude to be facing diagonally across stage towards MOUTH, fully faintly lit, dead still throughout except for single brief movement where [illegible]. Stage lights out when curtain up and unchanged throughout.

~~into ... birth into the world ... this world ... a tiny ... in a small ... what? ... girl? ... [illegible] ... baby girl in a small [illegible] ... named ... in the [illegible] ... what? ... [illegible] ... named ... no matter ... parents unknown ... [illegible] ... devilish work ... almost ... [illegible] ... nothing ... what? ... coming up to sixty ... coming up to 65 ... sixty-five? ... walking in a field ... when suddenly ... all went out ... [illegible] ... or standing ... or sitting ... or lying ... or kneeling ... mind ... whether standing ... or sitting ... and the mind~~ [illegible]

KLE
12.32

little thing

the downs? no

birth ... into this world ... the world ... of a tiny ... 5-pounds ... in a godfor- ... what? ... into this ... named ... girl? ... tiny little girl ... in a ... hole ... in the bog ... no ... named ... named ... in the bog ... he having ... parents unknown ... no sooner ... vanished into ... thin air ... devilish work ... almost ... 9 months later ... such as normally ... so no love ... speechless infant ... in the [illegible] ... nor indeed for that matter ... in the home ... at any subsequent ... time ... any of any kind ... nothing worthy of note till ... so usual affair ... sober ... what? ... sixty-five? ... coming up to sixty ...

Portraits.

—

An easy lazy length of limb,
Dark eyes and features from the south,
A short-legged meditative pipe
Set in a supercilious mouth;
Ink and a pen and papers laid
Down on a table for the night,
Beside a semi-dozing man
Who wakes to go to bed by light.

"Like as we are."

—

His Heart hath bled for me, when mine is sore,
And when my feet are weary, His have ble
He had no place wherein to lay His Head,
When I am weary, He was weary more.

A pair of brothers brotherly,
Unlike and yet how much the same
In heart and high-toned intellect,
In face and bearing, hope and aim:
Friends of the selfsame treasured friends
And of one home the dear delight,
Beloved of many a loving heart
And cherished both in mine, Good night.

—

9th May 1853.

Whitsun Eve.

—

The white dove cooeth in her downy nest;
Keeping her young ones warm beneath her breast:
The white moon saileth thro' the cool clear sky,
Screened by a tender mist in passing by:

Tearing, cutting, pasting, stapling

Sometimes the act of cutting is done literally with a pair of scissors, or by tearing out a page or part of a page. Christina Rossetti, for instance, wrote a poem titled 'Portraits' on 9 May 1853. It has two stanzas, but between the first and the second stanza a stanza-length passage has been torn from the notebook (SEE FIG. 6). It appears that either the second stanza is a second draft, the first of which was cut (Rossetti would have written the second stanza underneath the first on the left-hand page, then decided it was not right, cut it and rewritten it on the right-hand page), or, alternatively, the poem initially had three stanzas, the second of which was torn from the notebook.

Portraits.
An easy lazy length of limb,
  Dark eyes and features from the south,
A short-legged meditative pipe
  Set in a supercilious mouth;
Ink and a pen and papers laid
  Down on a table for the night,
Beside a semi-dozing man
  Who wakes to go to bed by light.

[*passage torn from the notebook*]

A pair of brothers brotherly,
  Unlike and yet how much the same
In heart and high-toned intellect,
  In face and bearing, hope and aims:
Friends of the selfsame treasured friends
  And of one home the dear delight,
Beloved of many a loving heart
  And cherished both in mine, good night.
9th May 1853.[13]

The poem has been published as such, but with only these two stanzas it makes a truncated impression. Of the two brothers mentioned in the third stanza ('A pair of brothers brotherly'), only one appears to get a portrait (in the first stanza). Although the title speaks of multiple portraits, the second one seems to have been removed and never replaced.

6 One of Christina Rossetti's poetry notebooks, with a missing stanza torn from the page on the left (Oxford, Bodleian Library, MS. Don. e. 1/7 pp. 66–7)

What happens more frequently is that not just one stanza is removed, but an entire poem, or several poems. W.H. Auden's notebook with early poems is a good example.

Before the poem 'The plane tree' at least a half-dozen pages have been torn from the notebook (SEE FIG. 7), leaving us with the enigma of what may have been written on those pages; why Auden thought it was necessary to remove them; whether it was immediately after he had written them or much later, as a celebrated poet, retrospectively flicking through his juvenilia and feeling ashamed of what he had written as a young man.[14] It also raises the question whether the public image of the poet would have been significantly different if the poems had become part of the Auden canon. His mother, Constance Rosalie Bicknell Auden, appears to have feared that the poet would destroy even more poems. On a card that is kept with the notebook, she wrote: 'These poems of Wystan are not to be destroyed – nor given to him. They can be entrusted to a librarian.'

Similar traces of torn pages can be found in a notebook with poetry by Edward Thomas, who was killed during the First World War in the Battle of Arras (9 April 1917) and is often counted among the so-called 'war poets' (SEE FIG. 8).[15] Again, it is hard to reconstruct what may have been written on these torn pages. But that does not mean they are completely forgotten. Archivists carefully describe even these 'vestigial stubs' and give them a place in the collation of the document – a description of how the leaves were folded, gathered and bound (SEE FIG. 9).

A truly remarkable case of scissoring out parts of a manuscript is Gerard Manley Hopkins's notebook with fair copies (transcribed versions incorporating previous corrections) of poems in various hands, which he collected as an undergraduate.[16] When he was studying in Oxford, in the 1860s, he collected thirty-one poems in a notebook. Thirteen of them are by his father, Manley Hopkins, and two of these are even in his father's hand. The other poems are by various writers he appreciated, such as Ralph Waldo Emerson, Oliver Wendell Holmes, Alessandro Manzoni, Dante Gabriel Rossetti, Ford Madox Brown, Vincent Stuckey Coles, Henry William Challis, and especially Digby Mackworth Dolben. The poems by his friends are marked by their

7 Vestigial stubs showing that pages have been torn from this poetry notebook by W.H. Auden (Oxford, Bodleian Library, MS. Eng. poet. c. 68, fol. 16)

The Plane Tree

Thou hast no birds upon thy boughs
Who build their cosy nests and sing
No fields of grass with ~~lambs~~ [sheeps] and cows
Who scream with joy when it is spring
No flowers, no brooks, no lovely skies
No stars at ~~night~~ [eve] ope ~~sleepy~~ [laughing] eyes

Thy home is in the roaring street
The songs thou hast are made by trams
The bitter tap of wearied feet
For sound of ~~dances made~~ [measures danced] by lambs
The skies wear ~~grey~~ [Drab] and sooty hues
Instead of ~~country [illegible]~~ [pinks, white] and blues.

Yet art thou richer, humble tree,
Than fifty thousand oaks or elms
~~For~~ [Tis] Men ~~would~~ [illegible] with smile ~~for~~ [at] sight of thee
So thy ~~faded~~ [for such] beauty overwhelms
I know, in heavens streets, yes there
Thou wilt be planted everywhere.

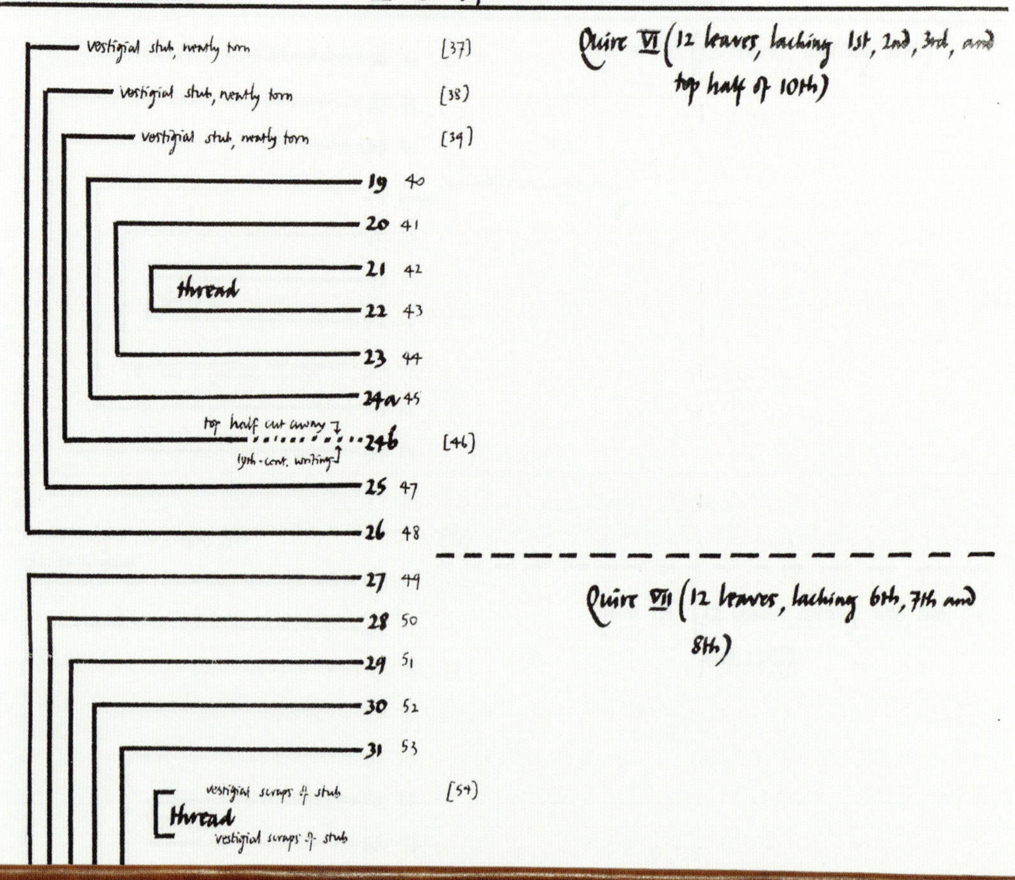

1.

C

25 VI 15 Hucclecote.

101

I built myself a house of glass:
It took me years to make it;
And I was proud. But now, alas!
Would God some one would break it.

But it looks too magnificent.
No neighbour casts a stone
From where he dwells, in tenement
Or palace of glass, alone.

initials only, not their full names. Coles, Challis and Dolben were part of the group of male friends who shared Hopkins's intense religious conviction. Especially Dolben had a significant emotional impact on Hopkins,[17] but not for very long. This also appears to be reflected in the notebook, for after thirty-one poems (including four by Dolben) the miscellany ends rather abruptly, leaving almost fifty folios blank. Instead of continuing the way he was living up until then, mimicking his contemporaries by copying out their poems, in 1868 Hopkins decided to devote his life to God and become a Jesuit. The notebook gives a unique insight into Hopkins's poetical interests preceding this moment, showing movement from a preoccupation with his father's work to a fascination with (notably) Dolben's.

Particularly in the first part of the notebook, Hopkins's father is by far the most dominant presence. Against this backdrop, it is remarkable that he scissors out his father's name underneath his poems and writes his father's initials ('M.H.') next to the cut-out parts. The cutting may at first sight seem an all too symbolic act of a son killing his father, which in Freudian theory might have been called an Oedipal act. But the father's identity is not entirely obliterated. His name is replaced by his initials. And since signing by means of initials was a sort of privileged treatment which Hopkins only reserved for his friends, one could argue that during this process of transcribing poems in his notebook, Hopkins's attitude towards his father developed from respectful but reserved reverence to a more relaxed ease that turned his father into a friend, before he eventually chose a life devoted to another Father: God.

Abandoned work, discarded pages

Keeping one's manuscripts is a relatively recent phenomenon. It also appears to be somewhat gendered. While the manuscripts of several male Romantic poets were revered as relics of their genius, those of a female novelist like Jane Austen (1775–1817) were to a large extent thrown away as soon as they were published. The manuscripts we do have are either juvenilia, abandoned works or alternative versions of certain parts (see Chapter 4). But even though they are not her most famous works, these manuscripts offer a rare glimpse into her creative process.

8 Vestigial stubs in a poetry notebook by Edward Thomas (Oxford, Bodleian Library, MS. Don. d. 28, fol. 1r)

9 Collation of Edward Thomas's notebook (Oxford, Bodleian Library, MS. Don. d. 28)

~~I am to suppose~~
"~~Your Mama is a compliment of your way~~, Lord said
~~Emma bowing, tho' I do not exactly understand it.~~"
~~Lord Osborne laughed rather awkwardly, & then said~~
"~~Upon my soul, I am a bad one for Compliments.~~
~~I wish I knew how to manage the matter~~
~~[illegible]~~
~~and after some minutes silence, added, "Can you~~
~~give me a lesson Miss Watson in the art of paying~~
~~Compts. I should be very glad to learn." "I want~~
~~a cold monosyllable, & gravely looks from Emma~~
~~[illegible] to know how to please the Ladies~~
~~repressed the [illegible]~~
~~and Lord Osborne~~ freedom of his manner.
~~He had too much sense not to take the hint~~ —
~~& when he spoke again, it was with a degree~~
~~of calm & decent propriety which he had never used~~
~~before that he [illegible] employing. He was rewarded~~
by a gracious answer, & a more liberal full view
of her face than she had yet bestowed. ~~[illegible]~~
Unused to exert himself, & happy in contem-
-plating her, he then sat in silence for ~~about five~~ some
minutes longer, while Tom Musgrave was chatter-
-ing to Eliz:th, till they were interrupted by Nanny's
approach, who ~~putting~~ half opening the door & putting
in her head, said "Please Ma'am, Master wants
to know why he be'nt to have his dinner."—
The Gentlemen, who had hitherto disregarded every
symptom, however positive, of the nearness of that
meal, now jumped up with apologies, while

Austen abandoned her novel *The Watsons* probably after her father's death in January 1805. The heroine of the story, Emma Watson, is the youngest daughter of a widowed clergyman with six children. At a ball in the nearby town she is sitting next to the young Lord Osborne, who – 'after hard labour of mind' – manages to start a rather awkward conversation about the weather. When Emma replies that she has not been out walking that morning because of the bad weather, he replies that she should wear half-boots or, even better, ride on horseback (SEE FIG. 11). The conversation runs as follows:

> 'Ladies should ride in dirty weather. – Do you ride?'
> 'No my lord.'
> 'I wonder [why] every Lady does not. ~~Ride~~. – A woman never looks better than on horseback. –'
> 'But every woman may not have the inclination, or the means.'
> 'If they knew how much it became them, they would all have the inclination – & I fancy Miss Watson – when once they had the inclination, the means would soon follow.'[18]

On the back of the page, Austen wrote the continuation of this conversation but appears to have had trouble developing it. She crossed out almost all the text on the first half of the page (SEE FIG. 10). This is what Austen wrote before she decided to cut it: Emma replies that she is probably to suppose that Lord Osborne means a compliment, but she does 'not exactly understand it'. Austen gently pushes the embarrassment further: 'Lord Osborne laughed rather awkwardly – & then said "Upon my Soul, I am a bad one for Compliments. Nobody can be a worse hand at it than myself."' Then Austen inserts an uneasy silence of 'some minutes' and keeps building up the embarrassment by letting him add insult to injury: 'Cannot you give me a lesson Miss Watson on the art of paying Compliments. – I should be very glad to learn. I want very much to know how to please the Ladies. – one Lady at least.' Between the lines, Austen then intervenes: 'A cold monosyllable & grave look from Emma repressed the growing freedom of his manner.'[19]

Austen crossed out this entire passage and pinned a patch of paper to it to cover it (SEE FIG. 11), replacing the fragment with the following continuation of the conversation, starting with Emma's reply to Lord Osborne's awkward suggestion that, if women knew how well they looked

10 Deletions in Jane Austen's manuscript of *The Watsons* (Oxford, Bodleian Library, MS. Eng. e. 3764, fol. 31r)

he had nothing more to say for some time
& could only gratify his Eye by occasional
glances at his fair neighbour. — Emma was no
inclined to give herself much trouble for his
Entertainment — & after hard labour of min
he produced the remark of its being a very
fine day, & followed it up with the questi
of, "Have you been walking this morning
"No, my Lord. We thought it too dirty." "You
should wear half-boots." After another pause
"Nothing sets off a neat ancle more than a
half-boot; nankin galoshed with black look
very well. — Dont you like Half-boot
"Yes — but unless they are so stout as to in
:jure their beauty, they are not fit for
Country walking." "Ladie
should ride in dirty weather. — Do you rid
"No my Lord." "I wonder every Lady doe
not. — A woman never looks bette
than on horseback." — "But every woma
may not have the inclination, or the mea
"If they knew how much it became them, th
would all have the inclination — & I fan
Miss Watson — when once they had the in
:clination, the means wd soon follow.

11 Jane Austen's manuscript of *The Watsons*, patch pinned to quire 7 (Oxford, Bodleian Library, MS. Eng. e. 3764, fol. 30r)

your Lordship thinks, we always have our own
ay. — That is a point on which Ladies & Gentle:
ave long disagreed — But without pretending to
ecide it, I may say that there are some circum:
tances which even Women cannot controul. —
male Economy will do a great deal my Lord, but it cannot
rn a small income into a large one." — Ld. Osborne
as silenced. Her manner had been neither sententious
 sarcastic, but there was a something in its mild
riousness, as well as in the words themselves
 which made his Lordship think; — and when he
ddressed her again, it was with a degree of considerate propriety, to
tally unlike the half-awkward, half-fearless stile
his former remarks. — It was a new thing with him
 wish to please a woman; it was the first time that
 had ever felt what was due to a woman, in
mma's situation. — But as he wanted neither Sense
r a good disposition, he did not feel it without
ffect. — "You have not been
ng in this Country I understand, said he, in the tone of a Gentleman. I hope you
 pleased with it." — He was rewarded by a

on horseback, they would all have the inclination to ride, and once they had the inclination the means would soon follow. Instead of letting the multiple embarrassment escalate, Austen now gives Emma the floor and makes her speak her mind:

> 'Your Lordship thinks we always have our own way. – <u>That</u> is a point on which Ladies & Gentlemen have long disagreed – But without pretending to decide it, I may say that there are some circumstances which even <u>Women</u> cannot controul. – Female Economy ~~may~~ will do a great deal my Lord, but it cannot turn a small income into a large one.'

The material aspect of the pinned patch has the extra effect that it physically covers the embarrassing scene, like a fig leaf. But Austen did not destroy the cut scene, she just provisionally hid it with an easily unpinnable patch. And the archive keeps both the fig leaf and the naked awkwardness underneath. It also keeps the rest of the manuscript. Whatever reason Austen had to abandon the novel fragment, she did not throw it away.

Samuel Beckett similarly abandoned some of his works. One of them was the first text he wrote in English again after having written in French for almost a decade. After the Second World War, he had been writing several stories, plays and novels in French, such as *Molloy*, *Malone meurt*, *L'Innommable* and *En attendant Godot*, when, in the middle of the 1950s, he felt like writing in English again. Since the end of the Second World War his style had developed very rapidly (in French), and when he started writing in English again it was as if his style picked up again where his English novel-writing had left off and his French novel-writing had begun, showing some correspondences with the psychological preoccupations in *Molloy*. Whatever Beckett's reasons for abandoning the work may have been, he did publish part of it, but emphasized its incompleteness in the title and openly presented it as what it was: *From an Abandoned Work*.

The Beckett archive at the University of Reading also holds fragments that were abandoned but never made it into publication. For instance, 'Last Soliloquy', a short dialogue between an actor *A* and a prompter *P*, rehearsing a suicide scene in a play (SEE FIG. 12). The focus of the action is on the moment the actor is about to drink poison from the goblet.

12 Samuel Beckett's manuscript of 'Last Soliloquy', torn from a ringed notebook (University of Reading UoR MS 2937)

P. The potion.

A. Where is it?

P. In your hand.

A. I have the glass in my hand?

P. The goblet. You enter with the goblet in your hand, say your piece, (quaff it) drop dead.

drain to the dregs/

A. All of a heap? crumble?

P. (reading) slowly to his knees, then forward on his face, lies prostrate & breathes his last.

A. Off we go. (Begins to swoon.)

P. Too soon. You swoon too soon. Can't swoon here. Not ripe.

A. And if I did? Who'd know?

(N) All man could — man can. Have with myself away. (Pause) all? No.

Not all./ (N.) Long pause & swoons.

No? Who'd know?

P. The author.

A. Fuck the author. Fuck all authors.

P. Are we sticking to the book or are we not. If not say the word & I'll leave you. (Pause.) Take it from the top.

A. (N) I have done. All I could — man can. All man can. Have with myself away. (Pause) all? No. Not all. Who can do all? What can any he did all. No. Not all. (Pause. fingers for prompt.)

P. (prompting) (Then what?)

A. (Then what.) If not all then what? What undone? What undone if not all done? Then what? (Pause. N.) Now what?

P. (prompting). What not if not —

A. (N.) Not what?

P (prompting) What not.

A. (N.) What not if not what not!

P. Right. Take it from what.

A. What what?

P. First. (P.) No. Not all. Long pause. What then?

A. What then. If not all then what? What undone? What undone if not all done? Then what? (Pause. N.) What not what not.

(Pause. N.) What you suppose that means?

P. What?

A. What not if not what.

The prompter repeatedly keeps the actor from fainting too soon, telling him that he 'Can't swoon here'. The actor defiantly asks him, 'And if I did?', wondering who would be the wiser, or who would know. When the prompter says 'the author', the actor replies violently: 'Fuck the author. Fuck all authors.'[20] But no matter how strong the fictional actor's feelings are towards authorship, it was still the author's prerogative to do with his unpublished text what he wanted. And Beckett decided to tear it from the ringed notebook he was using in the early 1980s (which served for other texts such as the English translation of *Mal vu mal dit – Ill Seen Ill Said* – and part of the first draft of *Worstward Ho*; SEE FIG. 13).[21]

13 Samuel Beckett's manuscript of *Worstward Ho*, torn from the same ringed notebook as 'Last Soliloquy' (University of Reading UoR MS 2602, fol. 1r)

WORSTWARD HO

Paris 9.8.81

A body. Where none. No mind.
That at least. / Where none. / A place. Where none.
For the body. To be in. Move in.
Out of. Back into. Nothing more.
A body & where none. No mind.
Where none. A place. Where none.
For the body. To be in. Move in.
Out of. Back into. No. In only.
Rot in. / Rot on in. / Stay in. / Nothing more. Back
all. Nothing all ~~[illegible]~~ [illegible] at all.

All before. Nothing else ever.
Ever tried. Ever failed. No matter.
Try again. Fail again. Fail better.

First the body. No. The place. First the
place. Where ~~[illegible]~~ none. ~~[illegible]~~

Ussy 12.8.81

No. Together. Now ~~[illegible]~~ the one. Now
the other. Stick with the one try the
stick / stick with / other. / with it back to the one. Sick
with either back sick with the other.
Till stick with both. Sick with both.
Puke & vanish. Where no place. No
body. Till sick with there. Then again.
A body. Where none. A place. Where
none. Fail again. Fail better again.
Fail better again. Till sick for good.
Sick for good. Fail for good. Puke
the last puke & vanish for good. Where
no more ~~[illegible]~~ more.

It stands. What? Yes. Stands. Stand
to get up in the end & stand. Yes.
Nothing for it in the end but get up
& stand. ~~[illegible]~~ The ground. The
ground or floor ~~it~~ whatever, it is hard as
iron. ~~[illegible]~~ No mind &
say / pain. ~~[illegible]~~ yet for the bones to
pain till it has to stand. Get up somehow
say / & stand. Or just enough. / Just enough
mind for pain. In that case for the bones
to pain all positions sitting & lying till
it has to get up somehow & stand.
~~[illegible]~~ & stand. ~~[illegible]~~ Provided pain.
Have of bones. Other examples later.
Of pain. Relief from pain. Then [illegible]
relief. ~~[illegible]~~
~~[illegible]~~
~~[illegible]~~
~~[illegible]~~
~~[illegible]~~
~~[illegible]~~ Murder stops. Comes
~~again~~ Murder again. Have how no
choice in the end but get up and stand.
Get up somehow & somehow stand.
No question. No mind for that. Just
no choice. That or scream. The scream to
be choice.

"You [illegible] a compliment of [illegible]," said [illegible]

[illegible] though I [illegible] understand it.

Lord Osborne laughed rather awkwardly, & then said

"Upon my soul, I am a bad one for compliments.

[illegible]"

[illegible]

and after some minutes silence, added [illegible]

[illegible] upon Miss Watson without offering

Compt: [illegible] should be very glad to be [illegible]

[illegible]

[illegible]

[illegible]

[illegible] Freedom of his manners.

He had too much sense not to take the hint —

& when he spoke again, it was with a degree

of [illegible] propriety which he had never used

before. [illegible] complying [illegible]

by a gracious answer, & a more liberal full view

of her face than she had yet bestowed. [illegible]

Unused to exert himself, & happy in contem:

:plating her, he then sat in silence for some

minutes longer, while Tom Musgrave was chatter:

:ing to Eliz:, till they were interrupted by Nanny's

half [illegible] the door & putting

2

REVISING

R.

Warning.

When I am an old woman I shall wear purple
And with a red hat which doesn't go, & doesn't suit me,
And I shall spend my pension on brandy & summer gloves
And satin sandals, & say we've no money for butter.
I shall sit down on the pavement when I'm tired
And gobble up samples in shops & press alarm bells
And run my stick along the public railings
And make up for the sobriety of my youth.
I shall go out in my slippers in the rain
And pick the flowers in other people's gardens
And learn to spit.

You can wear terrible shirts & grow more fat
And eat three pounds of sausages at a go
Or only bread & pickle for a week
And hoard pens & pencils & beermats & things in boxes.

~~But meanwhile we must stay respectable~~
~~And must not shame the children; they mind more~~
~~Even than we do, being noticeable.~~
~~We will keep dry with sensible clothes & spend~~
~~According to good value & do what's best~~
~~To bring the best for us & for our children.~~

But now we must have clothes that keep us dry
And pay our rent & not swear in the street
And set a good example for the children.
We must have friends to dinner & read the papers.

But maybe I ought to practise a little now?
So people who know me are not too shocked & surprised
When suddenly I am old & start to wear purple.

– November 2–4th, 1961

Listener Winter 1962

In literary drafts, a cut is often compensated by a substitution. If a deleted passage is a form of impasse, the act of crossing out is less negative than it may look. It can mark the realization that the writing was not exactly leading in the right direction. So cutting may be a way of moving on. Some poems have become so beloved and memorized by so many that it is hard to imagine they once existed in other versions.

Rewriting

'Warning' by Jenny Joseph (1932–2018) is such a poem. She wrote it between 2 and 4 November 1961, and first published it in the newsletter of the old people's home where her husband was working at the time, and then in *The Listener* (Winter 1962). The draft is written in a notebook kept at the Bodleian's Special Collections (see fig. 14). It opens as follows:

> When I am an old woman I shall wear purple
> ~~And~~ With a red hat which doesn't go, & doesn't suit me,
> And I shall spend my pension on brandy & summer gloves
> And satin sandals, & say we've no money for butter.
> I shall sit down on the pavement when I'm tired
> And gobble up samples in shops & press alarm bells
> And run my stick along the public railings
> And make up for the sobriety of my youth.
> I shall go out in my slippers in the rain
> And pick the flowers in other people's gardens
> And learn to spit.[22]

The poem continues enumerating for another stanza all the so-called inappropriate things she might do in old age, which is then followed by a new

14 Revisions to the second half of Jenny Joseph's manuscript of 'Warning' (Oxford, Bodleian Library, MS. 12404/41)

stanza starting with a 'But', marking a volta. In the published version this stanza reads as follows:

> But now we must have clothes that keep us dry
> And pay our rent and not swear in the street
> And set a good example for the children.
> We must have friends to dinner and read the papers.[23]

This 'But now' stanza, however, used to be different in the manuscript:

> But meanwhile we must stay respectable
> And must not shame the children; they mind more
> Even than we do, being noticeable.
> We will keep dry with sensible clothes & spend
> According to good value & do what's best
> To bring the best for us & for our children.

In her notebook, Jenny Joseph crossed out this version and wrote the alternative version next to it in the right margin in black ink, making one final change in blue ballpoint pen: 'We will have friends to dinner' became the even more oppressive bourgeois imperative, criticized in the simplest wording: 'We must have friends to dinner'.

The second volta was already present from the start: the first 'But' is followed by a second one, opening the final stanza with the gently rebellious half-smile dressed in a purplish question: 'But maybe I ought to practise a little now?'

Pencilling and overwriting

A less ironic form of practising is the old hands-on exercise of learning how to write as a child by first writing the letters in pencil before overwriting them in ink. J.R.R. Tolkien (1892–1973) applied this technique even when he was an established writer.[24] Take the moment in *The Lord of the Rings* when Frodo Baggins and his sidekick Samwise Gamgee approach Shelob's Lair in the chapter titled 'The Stairs of Cirith Ungol' (*The Two Towers*, book IV, ch. 8).[25] The rare manuscript page shows Tolkien's visually appealing way of revising. He first wrote the text in pencil, then sketched the scene halfway down the page before continuing with the story. The next step was to overwrite the text in ink, making

15 J.R.R. Tolkien's 'Shelob's Lair', first draft of Book 4, chapter 8, 'The Stairs of Cirith Ungol' of *The Lord of the Rings* (Oxford, Bodleian Library, MS. Tolkien Drawings 81)

'That's that!' said Sam. 'What we expected. But I don't like it. I suppose now we are just exactly where he wanted to bring us. Well, let's get moving away as quick as we can. The ~~has~~ headache's worn! That last whistle of his wasn't pure joy at getting out of the tunnel. It was pure wickedness of some sort. And what sort we'll soon know.'

'Likely enough,' said Frodo. 'But we could not have got even so far without him.' 'So if we ever manage our errand, then Gollum and all his wickedness will be part of the plan.'

'So far you say,' said Sam. 'How far? Where are we now?'

'About at the crest of the main range of Ephel Dúath I guess,' said Frodo. 'Look!' The road opened out now: it still went on up, but no longer steeply. Beyond and ahead there was an ominous glare in the sky; and like a great notch in the mountain wall a cleft was outlined against it so. On their right the wall of rock fell away and the road widened till it had no brink. Looking down Frodo saw only ~~but~~ the vast darkness of the great ravine that was the head of Morghul dale. Down in its depths was the faint glimmer of the wraith-road that led over the Morghul pass far below. On their left sharp jagged pinnacles stood up like towers carved by the bitter years, and between them were many dark crevices and clefts. But high up on the left side of the cleft to which they were bound (to the right) was a small black tower, and in it a window showed a red light.

'I don't like the look of that,' said Sam. 'This upper pass is guarded too. D'you remember he never would say if there was or no. D'you think he's gone to fetch them — orcs or something?'

'No, I don't think so,' said Frodo. 'He is up to no good, of course, but I don't think that he's gone to fetch orcs. Whatever it is, he is no slave of the Dark Lord.' 'I suppose not,' said Sam. 'No ~~I suppose at~~ the whole time it has been the way for poor Sméagol can. That's been his scheme. But how coming up here will help him, I can't guess.' He was soon to learn.

Frodo went forward now — the last lap — and he exerted all his strength. He felt that if once he could get to the saddle of the pass and look over into the Nameless Land he would have accomplished something. Sam followed. He sensed evil all round him. He knew that they had walked into some trap, but what? He had sheathed his sword, but now he drew it in readiness. He halted for a moment, and stooped to pick up his staff with his left hand

some small corrections. Finally the whole page of text is crossed through to show that this version was superseded (SEE FIG. 15).

The text on the page opens with Sam saying: 'That's that!' In the next sentence 'we' is replaced by 'I': 'What ~~we~~ I expected'. Sam asks: 'Where are we now?' 'About at the crest of the mountain range Ephel Duath, I guess, said Frodo. Look!' Tolkien then starts describing the landscape:

> The road opened out now: it still went on up, but no longer sheerly. Beyond and ahead there was an ominous glare in the sky, and like a great notch in the mountain wall a cleft was outlined against it – so[26]

That is where Tolkien starts describing the landscape in more detail, both with words and with a drawing:

> On their right the wall of rock fell away and the road widened till it had no brink. Looking down Frodo saw nothing but the vast darkness of the great ravine which was the head of Morghul dale. Down in its depths was the faint glimmer of the wraith-road that led over the Morghul pass from the city.

At least part of the text appears to have been written after he made the drawing. After the line 'On their left sharp jagged pinnacles stood up like towers carved by the', the text is draped around the image in the narrow space that is left to the right of it:

> biting years, and between them were many dark crevices and clefts. But high up on the left side of the cleft to which their road led (K. Ungol) was a small black tower, and in it a window showed a red light.[27]
>
> 'I don't like the look of that said Sam. This upper pass is guarded too. D'you remember he never would say if it was or no. D'you think he's gone to fetch them – orcs or something?
>
> No, I don't think so, said Frodo. He is up to no good, of course, but I don't think that he's gone to fetch orcs. Whatever he is, he's no slave of the Dark Lord.

This short dialogue between Sam and Frodo is one of the few passages of the manuscript fragment that is (more or less) retained in the published version:

'Do you remember he never would say if this pass was guarded or no? And now we see a tower there – and it may be deserted, and it may not. Do you think he's gone to fetch them, Orcs or whatever they are?'

'No, I don't think so,' answered Frodo. 'Even if he's up to some wickedness, and I suppose that's not unlikely. I don't think it's that: not to fetch Orcs, or any servants of the Enemy.'[28]

The pencil caption underneath the sketch notes that it is a rendering of 'SHELOB'S LAIR'. Apart from a red pencil, the drawing tools are mainly the same as Tolkien's writing tools: black ink and grey pencil.

Erasing: 'Whereof one cannot speak'

The habit of writing in pencil first also characterizes the draft of the *Tractatus Logico-Philosophicus* by the Austrian philosopher Ludwig Wittgenstein (1889–1951), a philosophical work that deals with the relationship between language and reality and tries to define the limits of science. It was written in German, when Wittgenstein was a soldier during the First World War. Unlike Tolkien, Wittgenstein did not overwrite his pencilled words with ink, but the use of pencil enabled him to easily revise and rewrite without creating too much chaos on the page. As in the case of the poetry notebooks of W.H. Auden or Edward Thomas, Wittgenstein seems to have removed a failed first attempt by tearing the first page from his notebook. But then he started writing his propositions in pencil, in his systematic, numbered way (SEE FIG. 16):

1 Die Welt ist alles was der Fall ist.
[The world is everything that is the case.]
1.1 Die Welt ist die Gesamtheit der Tatsachen, nicht der Dinge.
[The world is the totality of facts, not of things.][29]

Wittgenstein's method of numbering his propositions makes the act of cutting more visible in another way. There are seven main propositions or statements, subdivided into substatements. In the pencil draft, the number of substatements was still limited. For instance, in the published version, statement 6 is subdivided into five substatements (6.1, 6.2, 6.3, 6.4, 6.5) and each of them is further subdivided into more detailed ones (6.12, 6.122, 6.1221). In the draft, some of the pencilled propositions, such as the line above 6.4, were erased – another type of cut. The number of main statements is also seven in

OVERLEAF

16 Ludwig Wittgenstein's pencil draft of *Tractatus Logico-Philosophicus*, opening page (Oxford, Bodleian Library, MS. German d. 6, fol. 03r)

17 Ludwig Wittgenstein, pencil draft of *Tractatus Logico-Philosophicus* with erased lines (Oxford, Bodleian Library, MS. German d. 6, fol. 37v)

1 Die Welt ist alles was der Fall ist.

1·1 Die Welt ist die Gesamtheit der Tatsachen, nicht der Dinge

2 Was der Fall ist, die Tatsache, ist das Bestehen von Sachverhalten

2·1 Die Tatsachen begreifen wir in Bildern

2·2 Das Bild hat mit dem Abgebildeten die logische Form der Abbildung gemein.

3 Das logische Bild der Tatsachen ist der Gedanke

3·1 Der sinnliche Ausdruck des Gedankens ist das Satzzeichen

3·2 Das Satzzeichen mit der Art und Weise seiner Abbildung ist der Satz

4 Der Gedanke ist der sinnvolle Satz

4·1 Der Satz stellt das Bestehen und Nicht Bestehen der Sachverhalte dar

4·2 Der Sinn des Satzes ist seine Übereinstimmung, und nicht Übereinstimmung mit den Möglichkeiten des Bestehens und nicht Bestehens der Sachverhalte

4·3 Die Wahrheitsmöglichkeiten der Elementarsätze bedeuten die Möglichkeiten des Bestehens und nicht Bestehens der Sachverhalte

4·4 Der Satz ist der Ausdruck der Übereinstimmung und nicht Übereinstimmung mit den Wahrheitsmöglichkeiten der Elementarsätze

5 Der Satz ist eine Wahrheitsfunktion der Elementarsätze

6 Die Allgemeine Form der Wahrheitsfunktion ist:

$$|N(\bar{p}), \bar{\alpha}, N(\bar{\alpha})|$$

6·4 Alle Sätze sind gleichwertig

7 Wovon man nicht sprechen kann, darüber muss man schweigen.

6·12112 Das sogenannte Gesetz der Induction kann jedenfalls kein logisches Gesetz sein, denn es ist offenbar ein sinnvoller Satz. – Und darum kann es auch kein Gesetz a priori sein.

6·3 Das Causalitätsgesetz ist kein Gesetz sondern die Form ~~x~~ eines Gesetzes

6·31 „Causalitätsgesetz", das ist ein Gattungsname. Und wie es in der Mechanik, sagen wir, Minimum-Gesetze giebt, – etwa der kleinsten Wirkung – so giebt es in der Physik *ein* Causalitätsgesetz, *ein* Gesetz von der Causalitäts-Form.

6·311 Man hat ja auch davon eine Ahnung gehabt daß es *ein* „Gesetz der kleinsten Wirkung" geben müsse, ehe man genau wusste wie es lautete.
(Hier wie immer stellt sich das Aprioristische als etwas rein Logisches heraus.)

6·32 Wir *glauben* nicht a priori an ein Erhaltungsgesetz sondern wir *wissen* a priori die Möglichkeit seiner logischen Form.

6·33 Alle jene Sätze wie der Satz vom Grunde, von der Kontinuität in der Natur, vom kleinsten Aufwande ~~[illegible]~~ ~~[illegible]~~ in der Natur, etc, etc. alle diese sind Einsichten

6.52 Wir fühlen, daß selbst, wenn alle m ö g l i c h e n wissenschaftlichen Fragen beantwortet sind, unsere Lebensprobleme noch gar nicht berührt sind. Freilich bleibt dann eben keine Frage mehr: und eben dies ist die Antwort.

6.521 Die Lösung des Problems des Lebens merkt man am Verschwinden dieses Problems.

(Ist nicht dies der Grund, warum Menschen, denen der Sinn des Lebens nach langen Zweifeln klar wurde, warum diese dann nicht sagen konnten, worin dieser Sinn bestand.)

6.522 Es gibt allerdings Unaussprechliches. Dies z e i g t sich, es ist das Mystische.

6.53 Die richtige Methode der Philosophie wäre eigentlich die: Nichts zu sagen, als was sich sagen läßt, also Sätze der Naturwissenschaft - also etwas, was mit Philosophie nichts zu tun hat - , und dann immer, wenn ein anderer etwas Methaphysisches sagen wollte, ihm nachweisen, daß er gewissen Zeichen in seinen Sätzen keine Bedeutung gegeben hat. Diese Methode wäre für den anderen unbefriedigend - er hätte nicht das Gefühl, daß wir ihm Philosophie lehrten - aber s i e wäre die einzig streng richtige.

6.54 Meine Sätze erläutern dadurch, daß sie der, welcher mich versteht, am Ende als unsinnig erkennt, wenn er durch sie - auf ihnen - über sie hinausgestiegen ist. (Er muß sozusagen die Leiter wegwerfen, nachdem er auf ihr hinaufgestiegen ist.)

Er muß diese Sätze überwinden, dann sieht er die Welt richtig.

Wovon man nicht sprechen kann, darüber muß man schweigen.

Schluss!

the draft, but there are fewer substatements than in the published version. For instance, in the published version there are several propositions between 6.4 and 7, such as: '6.44: Not *how* the world is, is the mystical, but *that* it is.' Or '6.522: There is indeed the inexpressible. This *shows* itself; it is the mystical.' Or '6.54: My propositions are elucidatory in this way: he who understands me finally recognizes them as senseless, when he has climbed out through them, on them, over them. (He must so to speak throw away the ladder, after he has climbed up on it.)' These are not yet part of the draft, which could be considered more like a bare-bones skeleton of the *Tractatus*. For instance, in the draft, 6.4 ('All propositions are of equal value') is followed immediately by 7: 'Whereof one cannot speak, thereof one must be silent.' – 'Wovon man nicht sprechen kann, darüber muß man schweigen' (SEE FIG. 17).

That famous seventh proposition is also the closing line of (the carbon copy of) the typescript held at the Bodleian (SEE FIG. 18). Underneath that final statement, Wittgenstein has written in pencil and with an exclamation mark: 'Schluss!' (The End!)[30]

Cancelling 'me'

In social media, indignation or offence often results in various forms of cancelling. Someone who is so often cancelled in literature that one can almost speak of a 'cancel culture' is the first-person narrator. Many stories or novels start with a first-person narrator, but after a few drafts the 'I' is cut and the story becomes a third-person narration. Evidently, the reverse also occurs, but the change from first- to third-person narration is remarkably frequent. A good example of both is the novel *The Castle* (*Das Schloss*) by Franz Kafka (1883–1924). After a brief false start of 3½ pages using third-person narration, Kafka wrote the first draft of what was to become the novel's opening sentence.[31] He drew a short line (SEE FIG. 19) and wrote: 'Es war spät abend als ich ankam.' ('It was late in the evening when I arrived').[32]

Barnabas, a messenger of the castle assigned to him, takes the narrator somewhere without him knowing where exactly. When Barnabas stops in front of his home, the first-person narrator wonders where they are. The text simply reads: 'Da blieb Barnabas stehen. Wo waren wir?' ('Barnabas stopped. Where were we?') (SEE FIG. 20).[33] This question is an example of self-narrated monologue. It is a way of conveying what goes on in the character's mind.

OPPOSITE

18 Ludwig Wittgenstein's typescript (carbon copy) of *Tractatus Logico-Philosophicus* (Oxford, Bodleian Library, MS. German d. 7, fol. 74r)

OVERLEAF

19 Franz Kafka's manuscript of *Das Schloss*, with a short line dividing the 'false start' from the beginning of the novel, and Max Brod's penciled note: 'Hier beginnt der Roman "Das Schloß"' (Oxford, Bodleian Library, MS. Kafka 34, fol. 2v)

20 Franz Kafka's manuscript of the novel *Das Schloss*, with the sentence 'Da blieb Barnabas stehen' at the start of the new paragraph just over the middle of the page (Oxford, Bodleian Library, MS. Kafka 34, fol. 20r)

~~Hand.~~ Das Mädchen entzog ihm langsam ihre Hand und sagte: „Du hast noch immer kein Vertrauen zu mir.“ „Mit Recht“ sagte der Gast und stand auf. „Ihr seid alle ein Pack“ „aber Du bist noch gefährlicher als der Wirt. Du bist eigens vom Schloß hergeschickt, mich zu bedienen.“ ~~Das Mädchen verlangte nicht~~ ~~Wie wenig Du unsere Verhältnisse kennst“ sagte das Mädchen und wiederholte dann~~ „Vom Schloß geschickt“ sagte das Mädchen „wie wenig Du unsere Verhältnisse kennst. Nur Mißtrauen fühlst Du“ „fort denn, nun fühlst Du wohl“. „Nein“ sagte der Gast, riß den Mantel von sich und warf ihn auf einen Sessel, „ich fühle nicht nicht einmal dieses: mich von hier zu vertreiben hast Du erreicht.“ Plötzlich aber schwankte er, hielt sich noch ein paar Schritte und fiel dann über das Bett hin. Das Mädchen eilte zu ihm: „Was ist Dir?“ flüsterte sie und schon lief sie zum Waschbecken und holte Wasser und kniete bei ihm nieder und wusch sein Gesicht. „Warum quält Ihr mich so?“ sagte er mühsam. „Wir quälen Dich doch nicht“ sagte das Mädchen. „Du willst etwas von uns und wir wissen nicht was. Sprich offen mit mir und ich werde Dir offen antworten.“

Hier beginnt der Roman „Das Schloß“ M.B.

Es war spät abend als ~~ich~~ K. ankam. Das Dorf lag in tiefem Schnee. Vom Schloßberg war nichts zu sehn, ~~ich blieb~~ ~~er war~~ Nebel und Finsternis umgaben ihn, ~~nicht einmal~~ auch nicht der schwächste Lichtschein deutete das große Schloß an. Lange stand ~~ich~~ K. auf der Holzbrücke die von der Landstraße zum Dorf führt und blickte in die scheinbare Leere empor.

Dann gieng ~~ich~~ er ein Nachtlager suchen; im ~~Der~~ Wirtshaus war man noch wach ~~aber~~ der Wirt hatte zwar kein Zimmer zu vermieten aber er wollte, von dem späten Gast äußerst überrascht und verwirrt, ~~mich~~ K. in der Wirtsstube auf einem Strohsack schlafen lassen, ~~ich~~ K. war damit einverstanden. Einige Bauern saßen noch beim Bier

der Wind spannte das Tuch, er blickte hinunter und in die Runde, auch über die Schulter hinweg auf die in der Erde versinkenden Kreuze, niemand war jetzt und hier größer als er. Zufällig kam dann der Lehrer vorüber, trieb K. mit einem ärgerlichen Blick hinab, beim Absprung verletzte sich K. am Knie, nur mit Mühe kam er nachhause, aber auf der Mauer war er doch gewesen, das Gefühl dieses Sieges schien ihm damals für ein langes Leben einen Halt zu geben, was nicht ganz töricht gewesen war, denn jetzt nach vielen Jahren in der Schneenacht am Arm des Barnabas kam es ihm zuhilfe.

Er hielt sich fester ein, fast zog ihn Barnabas, das Schweigen wurde nicht unterbrochen; von dem Weg wußte K. nur, daß sie nach dem Zustand der Straße zu schließen noch in keine Seitengasse eingebogen waren. K. gelobte sich, durch keine Schwierigkeit des Weges oder gar durch die Sorge um den Rückweg sich vom Weitergehn abhalten zu lassen; um schließlich weitergeschleift zu werden, würde seine Kraft wohl noch ausreichen. Und konnte denn der Weg unendlich sein? Bei Tag war das Schloß wie ein leichtes Ziel vor ihm gelegen und der Bote kannte gewiß den kürzesten Weg.

Da blieb Barnabas stehn. Wo waren sie? Gieng es nicht mehr weiter? Würde B. K. verabschieden? Es würde ihm nicht gelingen. K. hielt den B. Arm fest, daß es fast ihn selbst schmerzte. Oder sollte das Unglaubliche geschehen sein und sie waren schon im Schloß oder vor seinen Toren? Aber sie waren ja soweit K. wußte gar nicht gestiegen. Oder hatte ihn B. einen so unmerklich ansteigenden Weg geführt? „Wo sind wir?" fragte K. leise, mehr sich als ihn. „Zuhause" sagte B. ebenso. „Zuhause?" „Jetzt aber gib acht, Herr, daß Du nicht ausgleitest. Der Weg geht abwärts." „Abwärts?" „Es sind nur paar Schritte" fügte er hinzu und schon klopfte er an eine Tür.

Ein Mädchen öffnete, sie standen an der Schwelle einer großen Stube fast im Finstern, denn nur über einem Tisch links im Hintergrunde hing eine winzige Öllampe. „Wer kommt mit Dir, Barnabas?" fragte das Mädchen

Mit diesen zarten Händen" sagte K. halb fragend und wußte selbst nicht, ob er nur schmeichelte oder auch wirklich von ihr bezwungen war. Ihre Hände waren allerdings klein und zart aber man hätte sie auch schwach und nichtssagend nennen können. "Darauf hat damals niemand geachtet" sagte sie "und selbst jetzt –" K. sah sie fragend an, sie schüttelte den Kopf und wollte nicht weiter reden. "Sie haben natürlich" sagte K. "Ihre Geheimnisse und Sie werden über sie nicht mit jemandem reden, den Sie eine halbe Stunde lang kennen und der noch keine Gelegenheit hatte, Ihnen zu erzählen, wie es sich eigentlich mit ihm verhält." Das war aber wie sich zeigte eine unpassende Bemerkung, es war als hätte er Frieda aus einem ihm günstigen Schlummer geweckt, sie nahm aus der Ledertasche, die sie am Gürtel hängen hatte, ein Hölzchen, verstopfte damit das Guckloch, sagte dann zu K. sichtbar sich bezwingend um ihn von der Änderung ihrer Stimmung nichts merken zu lassen: "Was Sie betrifft, so weiß ich doch alles, Sie sind der Landvermesser", fügte dann hinzu "nun muß ich aber an die Arbeit" und ging an ihren Platz hinter dem Ausschanktisch, während sich von den Leuten hie und da einer erhob um sein leeres Glas von ihr füllen zu lassen. K. wollte noch einmal unauffällig mit ihr sprechen, nahm deshalb von einem Ständer ein leeres Glas und ging zu ihr: "Nur eines noch, Fräulein Frieda" sagte er, "es ist außerordentlich und eine auserlesene Kraft ist dazu nötig, von einer Stallmagd zum Ausschankmädchen sich emporzuarbeiten, ist damit aber für einen solchen Menschen das endgültige Ziel erreicht? Unsinnige Frage. Aus Ihren Augen, lachen Sie mich nicht aus, Fräulein Frieda, spricht nicht so sehr der vergangene als der zukünftige Kampf. Aber die Widerstände der Welt sind groß, sie werden größer mit den größeren Zielen und es ist keine Schande sich die Hilfe selbst eines kleinen einflußlosen aber ebenso kämpfenden Mannes zu sichern. Vielleicht könnten wir einmal in Ruhe miteinander sprechen, nicht von so vielen Augen angestarrt." "Ich weiß nicht was Sie wollen" sagte sie und in ihrem Ton schienen diesmal gegen ihren Willen nicht die Siege ihres Lebens, sondern die unendlichen Enttäuschungen mitzuklingen, "wollen Sie mich vielleicht von Klamm abziehn? Du lieber Himmel!" und sie schlug die Hände zusammen. "Sie haben mich durchschaut" sagte K. wie ermüdet von so viel Mißtrauen, "gerade das war meine geheimste Absicht. Sie sollten Klamm verlassen und meine Geliebte werden. Und nun kann ich ja gehn. Olga!" rief K. "wir gehn nachhause." Folgsam glitt Olga vom Faß, kam aber nicht gleich los von den sie umringenden Freunden. Da sagte Frieda leise, drohend K. anblickend: "Wann kann ich Sie sprechen?" "Kann ich hier übernachten?" fragte K. "Ja" sagte Frieda. "Kann ich gleich hier bleiben?" "Gehn Sie mit Olga fort, damit ich die Leute hier wegschaffen kann. Dann in einem

A more traditional way of telling this would have been direct speech, something like: 'I did not know Barnabas was taking me to his home, so when he stopped in front of the house, I wondered: "Where are we?"' But Kafka does not employ the tag 'I wondered' and instead of the present tense he uses the simple past: 'Where were we?' This type of 'free indirect speech' is fairly common in third-person narratives, but rather unusual with a first-person narrator.[34] The problem with a past-tense first-person narrative is that it constantly struggles with the difference in time between the moment of the experience and the moment of telling it. In the example 'Where were we?', Kafka tries to efface the narrating self (the 'I' telling the story with hindsight), and focus only on the experiencing self (the 'I' living through the story). But the result is rather artificial, because he tries so hard to hide or efface the narrating self. In a past-tense third-person narrative it is easier to create the illusion of immediacy and efface the narrator. Moreover, a past-tense first-person narrative also seems to give away that all will be fine in the end – after all, the narrator can still recount the story and is therefore probably still alive. Whatever happened, it cannot have been so bad that he died, unless the narrator is talking from beyond the grave. With a third-person narrative it is easier for a writer to leave things in limbo and convey the typically Kafkaesque sense of estrangement and uncertainty.

That is why it was so easy for Kafka to change this first-person narrator 'Ich' / 'I' into a third person, 'K.' As a result 'Where were we?' became 'Where were they?' – free indirect speech in a third-person narrative – and all the instances where 'Ich' was mentioned were changed into 'K.' It is even possible to pinpoint the moment this happened in the draft: on folio 25r (SEE FIG. 21). The first line on that page still shows the trace of the initial 'Ich' (overwritten by 'K.'), whereas the last line on that page features 'K.' as the new 'experiencing self': '"Kann ich hier übernachten?" fragte K.' ('"Can I spend the night here?" K. asked.') The question is addressed to Frieda, the barmaid at the inn called Herrenhof. At the top of the page he flatters her by making a comment about her hands:

> 'Mit diesen zarten Händen' sagte ~~ich~~ K. halb fragend und *wusste selbst nicht*, ob ~~ich~~ er nur schmeichelte oder auch wirklich von ihr bezwungen war.[35]

The initial version (before the cancellations and substitutions) could be translated as:

21 The moment in the manuscript of *Das Schloss* where Kafka switched from the first person 'ich' to 'K.', and started replacing the first-person pronoun retroactively (Oxford, Bodleian Library, MS. Kafka 34, fol. 25r)

> ‘With those delicate hands’, I said half questioningly, *without knowing myself* whether I was only flattering her or was compelled by something in her.

This is one of the last instances of first-person narration in the draft. Here, the narrator talks about himself as if, even with hindsight, he does not know what he was doing. As a consequence, he may come across as unreliable. That would have given the novel a completely different spin as it would have shifted the attention from (the uncertainty of) the experiencing self to the (unreliable) narrating self. Together with the artificiality of the free indirect speech in a past-tense first-person narration, all these elements may have contributed to Kafka’s decision. Towards the end of the page he appears to have realized that the first-person narration became too artificial; he switched to third-person narration, went through the forty-two pages he had already written so far, and cut all the relevant first-person pronouns, replacing them with ‘K.’

The empire strikes back

As the example from Kafka shows, striking out just a few letters can sometimes have a huge effect. The Jamaican poet and screenwriter Evan Jones wrote a powerful poem titled ‘Song of the Banana Man’. In the first typescript version, which is kept at the Bodleian, it opens with the following stanza:

> Tourist, white man, wiping his face
> Met me in Golden Grove market place.
> He looked at my old clothes brown with stain
> And soaked right through with the Portland rain;
> He cast his eye, turned up his nose,
> He said, ‘You’re a beggar man I suppose.’
> He said, ‘Boy, get some occupation
> Be of some value to your nation.’

The rest of the poem is a strong reply to the tourist’s stereotypical and patronizing attitude. The banana man has his own way of doing things and is proud of it, too. But in this typescript the poem is entirely written in the white man’s spelling. In the next version (SEE FIG. 22) Jones made the banana man’s statement stronger by letting him *show*, rather than only *tell*, what he has to say. The content is enacted by the form, because Jones cuts the ending of the opening word. The white man is no longer a Tourist but a Touris’, stripped

22 Evan Jones’s typescript of ‘Song of the Banana Man’ (Oxford, Bodleian Library, MS. Evan Jones 32)

SONG OF THE BANANA MAN

Tourist, white man, wiping his face,
Met me in Golden Grove market place.
He looked at my old clothes brown with stain
And soaked right through with the Portland Rain,
He cast his eye, and turned up his nose,
And said "You're a beggar man I suppose",
He said "Boy, get some occupation
Be of some value to your nation."

I said "By God and this big right hand
You must recognise a banana man".

Up in the hills where the streams are cool
Where mullet and janga swim in the pool,
I have ten acres of mountain side
And a dainty foot donkey that I ride,
Four Gros Michel and four Lacatan,
Some coconut trees, and some hills of yam,
And I pasture on that very same land
Five she goats and a big black ram.

That by God and this big right hand
Is the property of the banana man.

I leave my yard early-morning time
And set my foot to the mountain climb,
I bend my back for the hot-sun toil
And my cutlass rings on the stony soil,
Clearing and weeding, digging and planting,
Till Massa sun drop back o' John Crow mountain,
Then home again in cool evening time
Perhaps whistling this little rhyme.

- continued -

Head down the hill to banana stand

Praise God and this big right hand
I will live and die a banana man.

Banana day is my special day
I cut my stems and I'm on my way
Load up the donkey, leave the land,
When the truck comes down I take a ride
All the way down to the harbour side;
That is the night when you, tourist man,
Would change your place with a banana man.

round

Yes, praise God and my big right hand
I will live and die a banana man.

The bay is calm and the moon is bright,
The hills look black though the sky is light,
Down at the dock is an English ship
Resting after her ocean ship trip.
While on the pier is a monstrous hustle,
Tally men, carriers, all in a bustle,
With the stems on their heads in a long black snake
Some singing the songs that banana men make,

Like 'Praise God' and my big right hand
I will live and die a banana man.

Then the payment comes and we have some fun,
Me, Zekiel, Breda and Duppy Son,
Down at the bar near United wharf,
Knock back a white rum, bust a laugh,
Fill the empty bag for further toil
With saltfish, breadfruit, and coconut oil,
Then head back home to my yard to sleep,
A proper sleep that is long and deep.

- continued -

Genesis

He was a young god
So he worked with furious abandon
Strewing his precious suns around
In largely useless galaxies

Grandiose in his use of mountains, water, sky,
But not merely bombastic
For the detail of the microscopic was ingenious
Beyond the imagination of his predecessors
And the uses, particularly, of form and colour ...

But he wasn't sure
Not quite sure, even when he had finished,
Especially then,

That he had solved such questions as
The relation of stability to change ...

Cycles of birth and death were a masterpiece
But they weren't, not quite ...

Yet, oh, the thing was beautiful
Turning and glittering and many-coloured
Infinite in all directions in space and time
And yet completely self-complete ...

But he wasn't sure

So, as a sort of flourish to his signature
An underline for curtain
He made an animal in his own image
Except of course, for the dimensions lost
Transferring from eternity to time

Genesis

Gave it [us] the last perception of his mind
The sense of incompleteness
The gap between the intended and the done
The utter sadness of magnificence not quite

He gave it [us] that
And then he turned away.

He gave us that
And asked of us perfection.
or And asked of it perfection

of his self-righteousness, pronounced in the banana man's way, rather than according to the white man's rules. The banana man does things his way, and has his own voice.

Jones also wrote a poem titled 'Genesis', in which he paints a portrait of the Creator as 'a young god'. Eager to prove himself and 'with furious abandon', he made mountains, water, sky and 'largely useless galaxies'. But even – or especially – when he was finished, 'he wasn't sure' if he had done everything right and 'solved such questions as / The relation of stability to change...'.

Jones introduces the element of divine doubt as the very occasion for creating man, 'an animal in his own image', giving it precisely that sense of incompleteness that he himself was struggling with, the 'gap between the intended and the done', the 'utter sadness of magnificence not quite'. In both the manuscript and the first typescript the final couplet reads:

> He gave it that
> Then turned away, and cried.

Then, in a subsequent typescript, he left out the final words 'and cried':

> He gave it that
> And then he turned away.

Jones considers replacing 'it' (the animal in god's own image) with 'us', and underneath the poem he writes a few alternative endings, turning god from a crying creator into a cruel craftsman, demanding of his creature what he himself failed to accomplish: perfection. Jones, as the god of his own creation, also remained in doubt until the very end (SEE FIG. 23), hesitating in pencil between using 'it' or 'us' for the closing lines:

> He gave us that
> And asked of us perfection.
> or
> And asked of it perfection

23 Evan Jones's typescript of 'Genesis' (Oxford, Bodleian Library, MS. Evan Jones 32)

~~[illegible]~~

~~"[illegible] my Lord" said~~

~~[illegible] tho' I do not exactly understand it."~~

~~Lord Osborne laughed rather awkwardly, & then said~~

~~"Upon my soul [illegible]"~~

~~[illegible]~~

~~and after some minutes silence, added, [illegible]~~

~~[illegible] without [illegible]~~

~~[illegible]~~

~~[illegible]~~

~~[illegible]~~

~~and Lord Osborne~~ freedom of his manner

~~He had too much sense not to take the hint —~~

~~& when he spoke again, it was with a degree~~

~~of considerate propriety, which he had never~~

~~before [illegible]~~

by a gracious answer, & a more full view of her face than she had yet bestowed. ~~[illegible]~~

Unused to exert himself, & happy in contem=plating her, he sat in silence for some minutes longer, while Tom Musgrave was chatter=ing to Eliz:th, till they were interrupted by Nanny's half [illegible] the door & putting

3
VESTIGIAL NOTES

2

TITLES

Twenty Minutes Sleep

Playback

The Quiet Ivories (Piano used for hiding body a la Stevenson)

Costume Piece

The Bearded Lady

Goldfish USED

Serenade before Twilight

See the Captain

Three Dead Detectives

Twenty Inches of Monkey (Monkeys bought for vivisection by inch—1$ per in.)

Uncle Watson Wants to Think

They Still Come Honest

Zone of Twilight

Between Two Liars (suggested by Cissy)

The Lady with the Truck

A Rolls in front of Sardi's

The Black-eyed Blonde

Parting Before Danger

Steel is the Color of Twilight

Jade USED

Rigadoo (A sort of fun festival to raise money for a worthy purpose)

Thunder Bug (Don't know what it means?)

The Is to Was Man (Killer)

Similes, etc.

As rare as a fat mailman (postman) (Cissy)

As shallow as a cafeteria tray

As meaningless as cheap laquer

As hard as a park bench (use in another sense)

As meaningless as a smoke ring

As dull as a football interview

As cold as a bride's dinner

As cold as a nun's breeches

As clean as Aunt Harriet's guest room

As clean asn angel's neck

As cold as Finnegan's feet

As slippery as a watermelon seed

As noiseless as a finger in a glove

High enough to have snow on him

As systematic as a whore

As busy as a dirty story in a sorority house.

As inconspicuous as a privy on the front lawn

Asncomfortable as a chiropractic treatment

As tight as a rubber stocking

As weak as a Chinaman's tea

As empty as a scarecorw's pockets (Used)

As fancy as a Filipino on Saturday night

As confidentially as a madam counting the take

Too weak to crawl over a worm

In biology, organs that once used to have a function but gradually atrophied are usually called 'vestigial' organs. For instance, some snakes, like the boa constrictor, have two small hook-like protrusions towards the back of their body. These do not have a function anymore, but they do indicate that, at some point in the species' evolution, they served as hind legs.

Similarly, in literature, there are numerous examples of 'vestigial' notes. They are kept in archives, even though they never contributed directly to any of the author's published works. For instance, after the publication of his famous novel *Ulysses* (1922), James Joyce (1882–1941) started filling dozens of notebooks with reading notes for his next project, *Finnegans Wake*. For this 'work in progress' he selected odd phrases from the most divergent texts. Whenever he used any of these phrases in his own work, he would cross it out with a coloured crayon to avoid using it twice. Joyce described this modus operandi as 'notesnatching' – another form of cutting, as it were: excerpting a phrase, separating it from its original context, and appropriating it by writing it in a notebook without reference to its author. In the new context of Joyce's notebook, every note is juxtaposed with other, often totally unrelated, notes. This juxtaposition created opportunities for Joyce to make associations between jottings that derived from various sources. Joyce himself saw this as a process of 'decomposition' for the purpose of 'recombination': the original context was decomposed and the snatched notes were recombined into a new text, titled *Finnegans Wake*. Many of these plundered phrases in Joyce's word hoard were crossed out in coloured crayon, but many more were never used. One could ask the question whether it is worth keeping all these notes that did not make it into publication, but then one should also wonder why authors themselves found it worthwhile keeping the vestigial notes in the first place.

24 Raymond Chandler's list of possible titles for books (Oxford, Bodleian Library, Dep. Chandler 1, fol. 02r)

25 Raymond Chandler's list of similes (Oxford, Bodleian Library, Dep. Chandler 1, fol. 07r)

‘Notesnatching’ and word hoards

Take, for instance, the American-British writer Raymond Chandler (1888–1959). He kept a ring binder with typed notes that served as a repository of ideas for his detective novels, such as lists of titles for potential novels (SEE FIG. 24):

> Twenty Minutes Sleep
> Playback
> The Quiet Ivories
> Costume Piece
> The Bearded Lady
> Goldfish

He marked the titles he had used, such as ‘Goldfish’ or ‘Jade’ (as in ‘Mandarin’s Jade’), by explicitly typing ‘USED’ next to them. That does not mean the others are irrelevant. It is interesting to see the alternatives from which he made his selection, and to see how he explains what he means by some of them, such as ‘The Quiet Ivories’, referring to a ‘(Piano used for hiding body a la Stevenson)’.

Chandler is famous not only for his hard-boiled style, but also for his original similes (highlighting the similarities between two things by using comparison words such as ‘like’ or ‘as’). Again, as with the titles, he made lists of similes (SEE FIG. 25), often crossing them out with a pencil and indicating whether (and where) he had used them – probably to avoid using them twice.

For instance, ‘~~As empty as a scarecrow’s pockets (Used)~~ The Big Sleep’ or ‘~~As cold as Finnegan’s feet~~ (used) Farewell [My Lovely]’. The unused or ‘vestigial’ similes may not have made it into any novel, but they did have a function in the creative process. Some of them contain racial stereotypes, but others are as evocative as a haiku, so to speak: ‘As shallow as a cafeteria tray’ or ‘As slippery as a watermelon seed’. Clearly, Chandler could only have become the simile expert he was by coming up with more similes than he needed and being selective.

Written souvenirs

Another writer who kept many of his vestigial notes was the British poet Ivor Treby (1933–2012), a professional biochemistry teacher and member of the Gay Authors’ Workshop. He was an authority on the writings of ‘Michael Field’, the pseudonym of British authors Katherine Harris Bradley and Edith Emma Cooper. In the 1980s he spent his retirement travelling extensively, a passion

26 Early draft of the poem ‘Bar Gongora’ (when it was still called ‘Pausing’), from Ivor Treby’s notes and drafts (Oxford, Bodleian Library, MS. Treby 15)

HOTEL HUSA

GRAN CAPITAN

AVENIDA DE AMERICA, 5 • 14008-CORDOBA • ESPAÑA • TELEF. 957 - 470250 • DIREC. TELEG.: HUSA • TELEX 76662 • GCAP.

PAUSING. ([illegible] 17)

for a single glass
of Manzanilla
i step from the sun
into the cool light
of the bodega

You turn from the casks
to wipe the metal
bar-top, brush away
split husks of peanuts
give me grave welcome

Sun on Puerta
Macarena, ~~this~~ the
~~cool oasis, nut~~ taste of sea, iodine & nut
shells underfoot, your
shy civility

this memory i
~~take from~~ keep of Sevilla
~~bring~~

(ict) 16 April 1987.

HOTELES HUSA Fundada en 1930

(incidents on 15th).
[written during drive to Cordoba, & visit of mosque.]

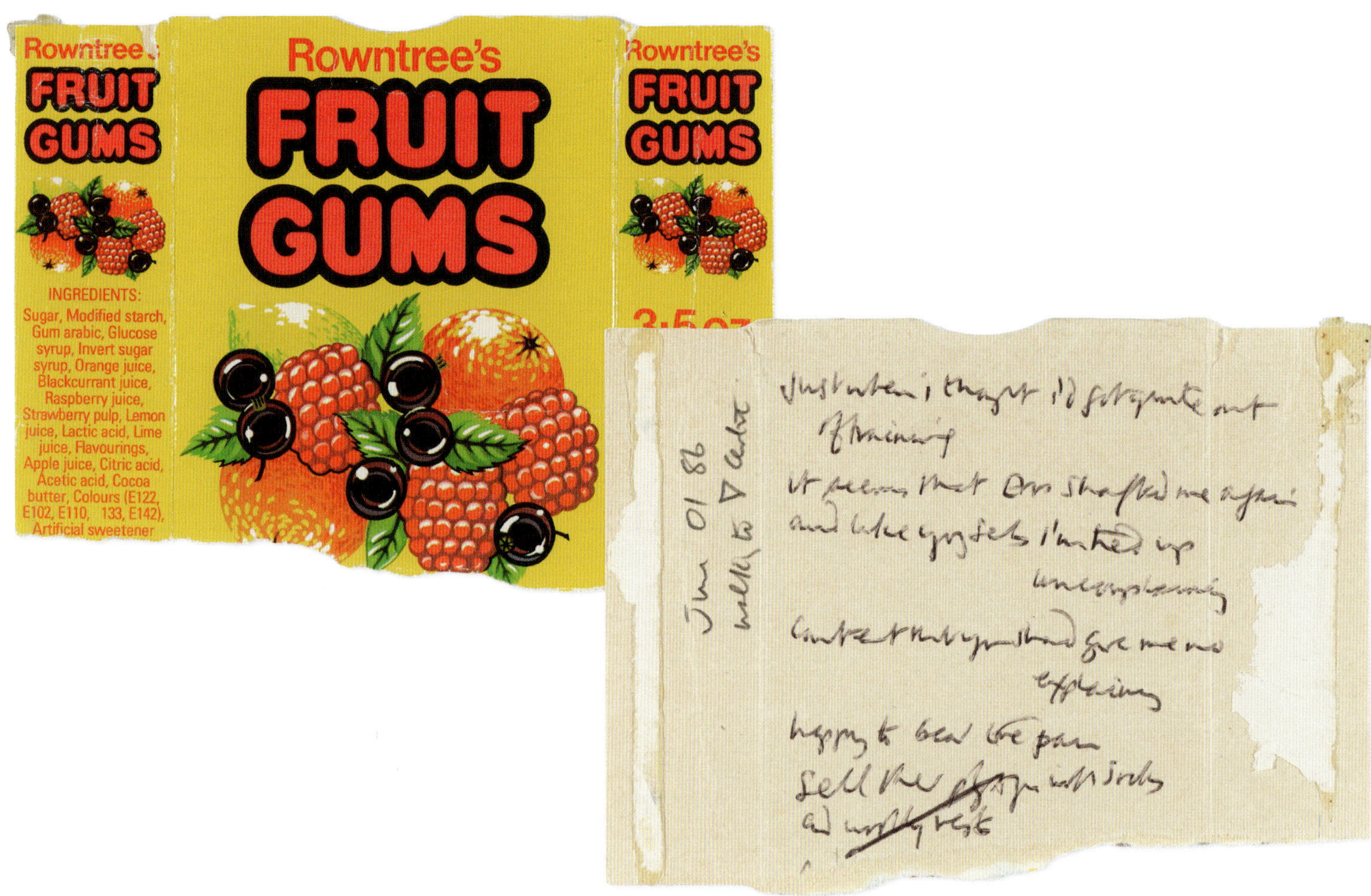

27 Ivor Treby's notes and drafts (Oxford, Bodleian Library, MS. Treby 15)

that is reflected in his poems. 'Bar Gongora', for instance (SEE FIG. 26), a poem published in *Gay and Lesbian Review* (September–October 2008, p. 17), takes the reader with him into the bar:

> for a single glass
> of Manzanilla
> i step from the sun
> into the cool light
> of the bodega

The 'you' that is introduced in the next stanzas is characterized by 'your shy civility', and the last stanza presents the poem as a souvenir: 'this memory I / ~~take~~ bring ~~from~~ keep of Sevilla'. The poem's original title was 'PAUSING'; it is written on stationery of Hotel Husa 'Gran Capitan' and dated 16 April 1987.

Not all of these written souvenirs made it into print. They were written on torn pieces of paper Treby happened to have in his pocket, such as the inside of a colourful packet of Rowntree's Fruit Gums (SEE FIG. 27).

Or a few drafts of a poem on Antwerp, jotted down on all sides of a folded piece of paper that Treby apparently had in his pocket while visiting the city in early January 1983 (SEE FIG. 28).

Starting with 'Jan 06 Ferry' we can follow the journey through several versions of a developing poem until it ends with a concluding version on a second sheet of paper, marked four days later, 'Jan 09–83 / journey back' (SEE FIG. 29):

> so you know Antwerpen?
> yes, i was there three nights
> hardly more than a weekend
> but long enough mind
> to explore and like it: that's
> often how things happen

He visits

> the Schelde, a great moat
> the Steen (Rubens of course –
> Van Dyck, the house of Plantin)
> the Brabo fountain
> in the Grote Markt, the bars
> on Van Schoonhovenstraat.

Again, the poem seems to serve in the first instance as a souvenir, concluding with: 'this I remember most / the warmth of the Flemish'. Treby's poems do not claim universality; they rather note the specificity of the fleeting moment. He even mentions the bars he went to by name – 'Boys Pub', 'Fifty-fifty', 'Scaramouche'. The *disjecta membra* of the poet's travels may be vestigial, but they did play a role in the creative development of his works. Treby carefully preserved most of these vestiges of the creative process in a brown envelope. With a thick black marker he wrote on the envelope, using a rather disquieting biological metaphor: 'FETUS & ASSORTED STILLBIRTHS!'

OVERLEAF

28 Ivor Treby's early draft of a poem on Antwerp (Oxford, Bodleian Library, MS. Treby 15)

29 Fair copy of Ivor Treby's poem on Antwerp, written on the journey back (Oxford, Bodleian Library, MS. Treby 15)

1-09 Tram booklet

So you know Antwerpen? 6
Yes i was there three nights 6
hardly more than a weekend 7
~~but enough mind~~ but quite enough mind 5
~~to fake it~~
to explain what it's like; truth 7
often how things happen 6

the Steen
the Schelde
Rubens Plantin
Plantin
the Grote Markt the Brabo fountain
the bars

in Van Schoonhovenstraat 6

Van Schoonhovenstraat
(5)

Jan 06 Jenny

where you live now friend
it is a warm house I can well suppose
and a cat perhaps you want the teacups
as you always planned
it is a warm house
and a cat perhaps

ANTONIUS

family 7

...th of the Flemish 6
...member most 6
...ning gay family
... and fifty-fifty
...y at Scaramouche 6
...us Antonius 7

...oyat Kirkel

...r most this -
... of the Flemish

Jan 09-83
journey back

6 So you know Antwerpen?
6 yes, i was there three nights
7 hardly more than a weekend
5 but long enough mind
7 to explore and like it: that's
6 often how things happen

6 the Schelde, a great moat
6 the Steen (Rubens of course -
7 Van Dyck, the house of Plantin)
5 the Brabo fountain
7 in the Grote Markt, the bars
6 on Van Schoonhovenstraat

~~seem to suppose.~~ 31

~~"You are a compliment of [illegible] my Lord," said~~
~~Emma bowing, tho' I do not exactly understand it.~~
~~Lord Osborne laughed rather awkwardly & then said~~
~~"Upon my soul, I am a bad one for compliments.~~
~~[illegible]~~
~~and after some minutes silence, he added, "Can you~~
~~give me a hint Miss Watson without affronting, I~~
~~should be very glad to have ... [illegible]~~
~~[illegible]~~
~~[illegible]~~
~~[illegible]~~ freedom of his manner.
~~He had too much sense not to take the hint —~~
~~& when he spoke again, it was with a degree~~
~~of considerate propriety which he had never used~~
~~before. [illegible]~~ [illegible]
by a gracious answer, & a more full view
of her face than she had yet bestowed.
Unused to exert himself, & happy in contemplating her, he then sat in silence for some
minutes longer, while Tom Musgrave was chattering to Eliza, till they were interrupted by Nanny's
half ... the door & putting

4

REPLACEMENTS & LATE SUBSTITUTES

The Mole + the Water Rat

by
Kenneth Grahame

1. The River Bank – say 5.000

2. The Open Road .. 5.000

3 The Wild Wood .. 5.000 (nearly ready)

(more to come here)

4. Toad's terrible Adventures say 5.000
5. The further Adventures of Toad .. 5000 } nearly [illegible]

Finis

Beginnings of
The Wind In The Willows
"The original Letters to his son"

Mrs Kenneth Grahame
16. Durham Villas
Campden Hill
W.

One of the most frequent types of cut is related to naming: finding a title for the work or giving the right name to a character. In 'The Philosophy of Composition' Edgar Allan Poe (1809–1849) explains how he wrote 'The Raven' – a narrative poem about a raven entering the window of a man lamenting the loss of his love, Lenore, asking the raven whether he'll ever see her again, the answer to which is the famous refrain: 'Quoth the Raven "Nevermore."' In his after-the-fact account of the genesis, Poe is eager to present his writing practice as an entirely rational enterprise, planned with mathematical precision. But then, very briefly, he does admit that when he was considering which animal could speak the pivotal word 'Nevermore', his initial thought was to choose a parrot. He claims he immediately dismissed the idea, but somehow, once the thought of a parrot has been admitted, it is as if the window has been opened again and the dark, gloomy atmosphere of this poem is disturbed by a colourful parrot, and no matter how hard the author of 'The Raven' may try to shut it up or chase it out of the window again, the stanzas suddenly end with a cheerful: 'Quoth the parrot "Nevermore!"' And the chirpy disturbance is complete when you realize that this would have meant that the bleak poem, opening with the line 'Once upon a midnight dreary, while I pondered, weak and weary', would not have been headed by the title 'The Raven' but by 'The Parrot'.

Changing titles and characters' names

Perhaps not as radical a change of tone, but a change nonetheless, happened during the writing process of *The Wind in the Willows* by Kenneth Grahame (1859–1932). At an early stage in the genesis the story's title was 'The Mole & the Water Rat' (SEE FIG. 30).

30 Kenneth Grahame's manuscript of 'The Mole & the Water Rat' (*The Wind in the Willows*) (Oxford, Bodleian Library, MS. Eng. misc. e. 247, fol. 1r)

31 Envelope containing Kenneth Grahame's letter with the beginnings of *The Wind in the Willows* (Oxford, Bodleian Library, MS. Eng. misc. d. 281)

Grahame wrote the book for his son, Alastair, whose nickname was 'Mouse'. On 10 May 1907, while Grahame was on a holiday in Falmouth, he wrote a letter to his son, who would be turning seven on 12 May (SEE FIG. 31).

That letter contains the 'Beginnings of The Wind in the Willows' according to a note on the preserved envelope. On stationery of the Green Bank Hotel, the letter opens:

> My darling Mouse,
> This is a birthday letter, to wish you very many happy returns of the day.

After having mentioned that 'Mummy has sent you some sand-toys to play in the sand with, and a card game', Grahame asks:

> Have you heard about the toad? He was never taken prisoner by brigands at all. It was all a horrid low trick of his. He wrote that letter himself – the letter saying that a hundred pounds must be put in the hollow tree. And he got out of the window early one morning & went off to a town called Buggleton & went to the Red Lion Hotel & there he found a party that had just motored down from London, & while they were having breakfast he went into the stable-yard & found their motor-car & went off in it without even saying Poop-poop! And now he has vanished & every one is looking for him, including the police. I fear he is a bad low animal.[36]

In the second 'Wind in the Willows' letter, for instance, Mr Toad is in prison, calling himself 'Base animal that I am' and 'O unhappy & ~~abandoned~~ forsaken toad' (letter 23 May 1907). In the story, Toad is imprisoned 'in the remotest dungeon of the best guarded keep of the stoutest castle in all the length & breadth of Merry England' (MS 172).

Obviously, the letters continue a storyline that the child was already familiar with. Grahame had the habit of telling his son bedtime stories as far back as early 1903, and so there is an oral origin that precedes these written 'beginnings'. Still, the letters did play an important part in the process of writing *The Wind in the Willows*. While Mr Toad is thought to have been partially inspired by Alastair, one of the models of the Water Rat is Sir Arthur Quiller-Couch, or Q, the man who gave aspiring writers the advice: 'Murder your darlings' in his lecture 'On Style' (see Introduction and fig. 32).[37]

32 Manuscript of Q's lectures: Sir Arthur Quiller-Couch, *On the Art of Writing*, lecture xii, 'On Style' (Trinity College, Archive, Oxford, DD36 Symondson/D/1)

To begin with, let me plead that you have been told – implicitly at any rate – of one or two things which Style is not; which have little or nothing to do with Style, though sometimes vulgarly mistaken for it. Style, for example, is not – can never be – extraneous Ornament. You remember, maybe, the Persian lover whom I quoted to you out of Newman: how to convey his passion he sought a professional letter-writer who, duly instructed, forthwith dipped the pen of desire in the ink of devotedness and proceeded to spread it over the page of desolation; whereupon the nightingale of affection was heard to warble to the rose of loveliness, while the breeze of anxiety played around the brow of expectation. Here, in this extraneous, professional, purchased ornamentation, you have something which Style _is not_: and if you require a practical rule of me, I will present you with this:– 'Whenever, being under the age of fifty (beyond which term experience has scarcely carried me) you feel an impulse to perpetrate a piece of exceptionally fine writing, obey it – obey it whole-heartedly – and tear it up before sending your manuscript to press. _Murder your darlings_ – I never promised you that a writer's was an easy life.

But let me plead further that you have not been left altogether without clue to the secret of what Style _is_. That you must follow the clue & master the secret for yourselves lay implicit in our bargain, & (I repeat) you were never promised that a writer's life would be easy. Yet a clue was certainly put in your hands when having insisted that Literature is a living Art, I added that therefore it must be personal and of its essence personal.

This goes very deep: it conditions all our criticism of art, – and of literature, which is an art; yet it conceals no mystery. You may see its meaning most easily & clearly, perhaps, by contrasting Science and Art at their two extremes – say Pure Mathematics with Acting. Science as a rule deals with things, Art with man's thought and emotion about things. In Pure Mathematics things are resolved into ideas, numbers, concepts. but

Quiller-Couch enjoyed boating, like the Water Rat or 'Ratty', who assures Mole that 'there is nothing – absolutely nothing – half so much worth doing as simply messing about in boats'.[38]

Grahame was a good friend of Quiller-Couch's and often stayed at his house in Fowey. Peter Hunt suggests that the homosocial atmosphere, especially in the chapters 'The Wild Wood', 'Mr Badger' and 'Dulce Domum', is 'suffused with a deep nostalgia for an England that was passing'.[39] Against this background, it is noteworthy that the title was initially 'The Mole & the Water Rat' – suggesting they are the actual protagonists, and that Mr Toad – as Grahame was quick to make clear to his seven-year-old son – was a bit of a nuisance, disturbing the Mole and the Water Rat's jolly English countryside idyll of messing about – not only in boats, as in Chapter IV, 'Mr. Badger': 'the Mole and the Water Rat, shaking off their garments in some thirty seconds, tumbled in between the sheet in great joy and contentment'. The title Grahame suggested to the London publisher Methuen was *Mr Mole and his Mates*;[40] Methuen, however, advertised the book as *The Wind in the Reeds*, but, as this was too close to W.B. Yeats's 1899 collection of poetry *The Wind Among the Reeds*, they settled for *The Wind in the Willows*.

Characters' names are also prone to changes. Take, for instance, the novel *Excellent Women* (1952) by Barbara Pym (1913–1980). The writing 'Started 19th Feb. 1949', as the manuscript indicates.[41] In terms of the setting, the novel takes place in England and, according to a pencilled note on the manuscript's first page, 'the time is February 1946' (SEE FIG. 33).[42]

The first-person narrator and protagonist is called Mildred Lathbury. Her character is described as a 'spinster without ties – inquisitive, willing to help others'; she has 'No life of [her] own'. Her position is characterized as 'An onlooker sees most of the game etc'.[43] Next to this pencilled characterization, Pym has written 'Clarissa', suggesting that that was the original name she had in mind for Mildred. The other protagonist, Helena Napier, also had a different name initially. In the first version of the opening line, her name is Daliers. Later, Pym crossed it out, pencilled the name 'Napier' above it, and 'Helena Napier' in the top right margin. A few pages further

33 Changes to character names in the manuscript of Barbara Pym's novel *Excellent Women* (Oxford, Bodleian Library, MS. Pym 14, fol. 1r)

The time is February 1946 it begins –

19th February 1949

Helena Napier

c 250 words per page

Chapter I.

~~Graham~~ Napier

I first met Mrs ~~Dakers~~ when I was taking the rubbish down one Saturday afternoon. The dustbins in the basement ~~were~~ shared by the occupants of the two flats in the house and as the ground floor was let as offices I generally avoided those hours when I might have the embarrassment of meeting a smartly dressed businessman ~~that when I was carrying a~~ laden with a bucket and waste paper basket.

"You must be ~~Miss~~ Cathbury", she said "I've seen your name on one of the door bells."

"Yes, I live in the flat above you." I

"I hope you've got comfortably settled in – moving is such a business, isn't it. It will be nice to have somebody else in the house" I ventured, for ~~the flat had been empty for some~~ during the last year of the war my friend ~~E Janet~~ Dora and I had been the only occupants, and I had been quite alone for a month since she had left to nurse her ~~old~~ mother, who had worn out two patient companions.

"Oh, well I don't suppose I shall be in much," said Mrs. ~~Dakers~~ Napier, quickly and bluntly.

"Oh, no," I said, drawing back "Neither am I." I quite understood her reluctance to pledge herself to anything that might become a tie or a nuisance. We were, superficially at any rate, a very unlikely pair to become friendly, although we must have been roughly the same age – in the middle thirties. But she ~~was~~ was tall, dark and elegant in well tailored slacks and I, mousy and rather plump in an old grey skirt and an overall.

"My husband will be coming out of the Navy soon", she went on. "I'm just getting the place ready"

"Oh, yes, I see." ~~I became even more humble~~. I began to wonder ~~how she had chanced to~~ what had brought her

34 Philip Pullman's map for *Lyra's Oxford* (Oxford, Bodleian Library, MS. Eng. c. 7801, fol. 39)

trees ↑

Mary Malone lives here

NORHAM GDNS

BANBURY ROAD

ST SOPHIA'S

UNIVERSITY PARKS

University Museum (& Pitt Rivers)

ST GILES

ST GILES

SOUTH PARKS ROAD

PARKS ROAD

MANSFIELD RD

ST CROSS RD

RIVER CHERWELL

MANOR ROAD

JOWETT WALK

HOLYWELL ST

LONGWELL ST

BROAD ST

N MUSEUM

NT ST

TREET

CORNMARKET ST

NEW INN ST

TURL ST

MARKET

HIGH STREET

QUEEN ST

MERTON ST

MAGDALEN BRIDGE

ST ALDATES

SPEEDWELL ST

STREET

BOTANICAL GARDENS

IFFLEY ROAD

JORDAN COLLEGE

OXFORD COLLEGES

A	Balliol	M	St Bernard's
B	Broadgates Hall	N	St Edmund Hall
C	Cardinal's	O	St Michael's
D	Durham	P	St Scholastica's
E	Foxe	Q	St Sophia's
F	Gabriel	R	Sanctuary
G	Hertford	S	Somerville
H	Jordan	T	University
I	Magdalen	U	Worcester
J	Merton	V	Wordsworth
K	Oriel	W	Wykeham
L	Queen Philippa's		

To Sir Charles Latrom's home ↑

on, Mildred's old schoolfriend is introduced as 'Dora Bodicote'. Her name later becomes 'Caldicote': 'It had so happened at that time that my old schoolfriend Dora ~~Bodi~~Caldicote had been wanting somebody to share her flat in London' (07r).[44] Pym then explains how, during the war, Mildred had started to work 'in the Censorship' – just like the author herself. Pym had been assigned to the Censorship Division of the Wrens in 1944.[45] With her witty sense of self-irony and without censoring herself, she writes what she thought about her work for 'the Censorship', 'for which, very fortunately, no high qualifications appeared to be necessary, apart from patience, discretion and a slight tendency towards eccentricity'.[46]

For people who grew up with the children's novel *Chitty-Chitty-Bang-Bang* by James Bond author Ian Fleming (1908–1964), it may come as a surprise that originally it did not start with 'Once upon a time there was a family called POTT'. It was almost the same beginning but the family name was different: Pough. The second sentence promptly explained that the family members did not pronounce it like the word *plough* but like *enough*. The fact that Fleming immediately felt the need to explain the pronunciation appears to have been a reason for changing the name. He replaced Pough by Pott, and described the family members, starting with the father, Commander Caractacus Pott, the mother, Mimsy, and a pair of seven-year-old twins, the black-haired Jeremy and the golden-haired Jemima.[47] Fleming wrote *Chitty-Chitty-Bang-Bang: The Magical Car* for his son Caspar. The novel was first published in three volumes, with illustrations by John Burningham, by Jonathan Cape in London in 1964.

Cutting names and replacing them with others may also have a more conceptual intention, as in Philip Pullman's fictional world, where the real and the unreal tend to mix. For *Lyra's Oxford*, he drew up a double list of colleges in two 'worlds', which is also relevant to *His Dark Materials* and indicates the interesting, minimal degree of deviation from reality he needed to create an entirely new storyworld. He also drew a map to give shape to this storyworld, where – for instance – Oxford University Press is replaced by The Fell Press (SEE FIG. 34).

THE COLLEGES OF OXFORD

in this world	*in Lyra's world*
University	University
Balliol	Balliol
Merton	Merton
Exeter	Jordan
Oriel	Oriel
Queen's	Queen Philippa's
New College	Wykeham
Lincoln	part of Jordan
All Souls	St Scholastica's
Magdalen	Magdalen
Brasenose	Sanctuary
St Edmund Hall	St Edmund Hall
Corpus Christi	Foxe
Christ Church	Cardinal's
Trinity	Durham
St John's	St Bernard's
Jesus	St Michael's
Wadham	Gabriel
Pembroke	Broadgates Hall
Worcester	Worcester
Hertford	Hertford
Lady Margaret Hall	St Sophia's
Somerville	Somerville
St Hugh's	Wordsworth[48]

Late revisions

Even at a very late stage in the writing process, authors often keep cutting and chiselling to make sure their work is presented to the public the way they want. W.B. Yeats, for instance, wrote a poem titled 'All Souls' Night' in the autumn of 1920, while he and his wife Georgie were living in Oxford in a house which used to be where the Bodleian's Weston Library is now (45 Broad Street). The poem was to be published in *The New Republic* (9 March 1921) and Yeats made quite a few changes to the typescript for the printer (SEE FIG. 35). In the typed layer of this printer's copy, the second stanza opens as follows:

ALL SOULS' NIGHT.

I.

It is All Souls' night and the great ChristChurch bell,
And many a lesser bell, sound through the room,
For it is now midnight;
And two long glasses brimmed with muscatel
Bubble upon the table. A ghost may come,
For it is a ghost's right,
His element is so fine
Being sharpened by his death,
To drink from the wine-breath
While our gross palates drink from the whole wine.

II.

I need some mind, that ~~should World beat on the ground~~ if the cannon sound
~~And blustering Time/all his shows can stay~~
From every quarter of the world, can stay
Wound in minds pondering,
As mummies in the mummy cloth are wound;
Because I have a marvellous thing to say,
A certain marvellous thing
None but the living mock,
Though not for sober ear;
It may be all that hear
Should laugh and weep an hour upon the clock.

I need some mind that should World beat on the ground
And blustering Time springs all his shows can stay
Wound in minds pondering
As mummies in the mummy cloth are wound
Because I have a marvellous thing to say
A certain marvellous thing

On the printer's copy, Yeats largely undid the first two lines and in blue-black ink he changed them to:

I need some mind, that if the cannon sound
From every quarter of the world, can stay

When the poem was published in the American journal, it was simultaneously published in *The London Mercury* of March 1921. In that version, the opening line was not 'It is All Souls' Night', but ''Tis All Souls' Night' – 'a little smidgin of good old-fashioned poetic diction didn't raise an eyebrow', as Paul Muldoon noted in one of his Oxford Lectures, when he was Professor of Poetry from 1999 to 2004.[49]

Yeats famously kept making changes to his poems, even when they were already published. In the case of this poem, after it had been published in *The New Republic* and *The London Mercury*, Yeats kept working on it. Instead of opening with 'It is…' or ''Tis All Souls' Night', he moved the third line up and started with 'Midnight has come'. It is always hard to speculate why a poet makes such a change, but as Paul Muldoon notes: 'It's worth pondering what might have been going on in Yeats's mind when he made these revisions, and to judge what might have been gained, or lost, in the process.'[50] The main gain he sees, or rather hears, is the mimesis of the tolling bell of Christ Church – just around the corner from Broad Street – in 'the predominantly spondaic metre'[51] of the new opening line, an insistent succession of metrical feet consisting of two stressed syllables:

Midnight has come, and the great Christ Church Bell
And many a lesser bell sound through the room;
And it is All Souls' Night.

This form of chiselling and polishing at a late stage in the creative process or even the epigenesis (the continuation of the creative process

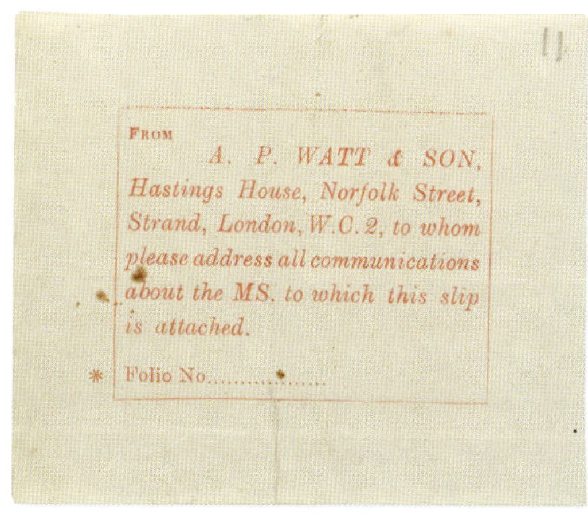
FROM A. P. WATT & SON, Hastings House, Norfolk Street, Strand, London, W.C. 2, to whom please address all communications about the MS. to which this slip is attached.

Folio No..........

35 Printer's copy of W.B. Yeats's poem 'All Souls' Night' (Oxford, Bodleian Library, MS. Don. c. 187, fol. 12)

A PORTRAIT OF THE ARTIST AS A YOUNG MAN

" Et ignotas animum dimittit in artes."
OVID, Metamorphoses, VIII., 18.

CHAPTER I

ONCE upon a time and a very good time it was there was a moocow coming down along the road and this moocow that was down along the road met a nicens little boy named baby tuckoo. . . .

His father told him that story: his father looked at him through a glass: he had a hairy face.

He was baby tuckoo. The moocow came down the road where Betty Byrne lived: she sold lemon platt.

O, the wild rose blossoms
On the little green place.

He sang that song. That was his song.

O, the green wothe botheth.

When you wet the bed first it is warm then it gets cold. His mother put on the oilsheet. That had the queer smell.

His mother had a nicer smell than his father. She

after publication) is not a prerogative of poets. Novelists do it too. A good example is James Joyce's *A Portrait of the Artist as a Young Man*. When the book was already published, Joyce made a list of corrections and sent it to his patron, Harriet Shaw Weaver. Weaver was editor of the magazine *The Egoist*, which had serialized *A Portrait of the Artist as a Young Man*: it appeared in twenty-five instalments between February 1914 and September 1915. The American publisher B.W. Huebsch published the finished novel on one of the last days of 1916 (29 December), and Harriet Weaver set up the Egoist Press to publish the book in the United Kingdom (SEE FIG. 36). She took a copy of the first English edition and inserted Joyce's corrections with a grey pencil. In a note pasted onto the original flyfleaf, she wrote that the corrections were 'sent by Mr. Joyce for the second edition, printed in Southport and published by The Egoist in 1917': 'They do not appear in the third edition (1921) for which sheets were again imported from the U.S.A. but they do appear in Mr. Jonathan Cape's edition (reset) of 1924.'[52]

The first correction is an addition to the beautiful opening:

> Once upon a time and a very good time it was there was a moocow coming down along the road and this moocow that was coming down along the road met a nicens little boy named baby tuckoo....[53]

But the corrections are sometimes also just cuts – not major cuts, but deletions nonetheless. Sometimes, they concern merely the omission of a punctuation mark, like the comma in 'When you wet the bed, first it is warm then it gets cold' (SEE FIG. 36). The comma is not just crossed out, but in the right margin it is also accompanied by a *deleatur* sign: ₰

As an editor, Weaver was well acquainted with the *deleatur* (from Latin, meaning 'let it be deleted'). The deletion of the comma may seem a whim of an overly fussy author, but it does make stylistic sense, since Joyce tried to write the opening scene from a young boy's perspective by making the style *enact* the boy's thoughts. And so, even this seemingly minor cut has a function.

In more recent fiction, the English travel writer and novelist Bruce Chatwin (1940–1989) was similarly concerned with textual details at a very late stage in the book's production process. In 1974 Chatwin left his job at the *Sunday Times Magazine* to travel to Patagonia in South America. The trip was the inspiration for his first book, *In Patagonia* (1977).

36 James Joyce's novel *A Portrait of the Artist as a Young Man* with late corrections (Oxford, Bodleian Library, Arch. AA e.97, p. 1)

The Bodleian holds almost all the papers relating to this book, from the many Moleskine notebooks he filled with impressions during his travels (SEE FIG. 37) to the final typescript, and even the 'Foldings & Gatherings'.

These 'F&Gs', as printers tend to call them, are what constitutes the book just before it was being bound: a pile of printed leaves, folded into quires or gatherings before they are sewn together. At that point in the production process, the author normally has already had the chance to correct (often two sets of) proofs. After this proofreading phase, the golden rule and silent agreement among printers and publishers is that 'F&Gs' are no longer shared with the author for fear that they might make even more changes at this late stage. But in the case of *In Patagonia* they seem to have made an exception for Chatwin, for he did get the chance to make a few final cuts and changes. On the last page, he cut the word 'most' in brown ink and replaced it with 'many' in this sentence:

> As we eased out of port a Chilean businessman played *La Mer* on a white piano missing ~~most~~ many of its keys.[54]

The typesetter wrote a blue check next to it to indicate that it had been corrected.

37 Bruce Chatwin's Moleskine notebook 1974–1975 (Oxford, Bodleian Library, MS. Eng. e. 3684)

Puerto Natales
Estancia Puerto Consuelo
Puerto Natales.
Mata Martinié
Maps Empresa Cousion.
Fiddley –
Skyping Water.

Nenu 26.2.72
Loco Mayannais en la Terre de
Jabon ~~de Castille~~
Dejeuner à la
Prickly Pear
~~Helena~~ lune fresca
Caja

P. Adamidi
021-51-
92
78

Tobchaftia Entenhijo

Tikotin

TUNA

Rio

Stream

new bridge

1st
16 March
18 Chiloe
Cantos
19 Bariloche
Laguna
Azul
20 Esquel
21 Esquel
Glacier in the

frozen fence

Campo

Trapiche

(212) 861-2789

casa

3 Rue du Lac
2550-1

Puerto
Harberton.

98 leaves

Audiobooks in the author's own voice create another opportunity for the writer to be confronted with their text, which sometimes leads to late cuts. For the audiobook of *Lyra's Oxford*, Philip Pullman made the obvious change in the preface from 'This book...' to 'This audio book contains a story and several other things.'[55] But during the reading, he also noticed the repetition of 'yet' in the following paragraph (SEE FIG. 38):

> Voices beyond the lower door: two men leaving Dr Polstead's room. Visitors – the university term hadn't ~~yet~~ begun, and he wouldn't be holding tutorials yet.

The occasion of the audiobook production was an opportunity to make that late cut.

38 Philip Pullman's annotated reading copy for the audiobook *Lyra's Oxford* (Oxford, Bodleian Library, MS. Eng. c. 7801, fol. 246)

the dæmon and the V-shaped patch of white feathers on his rump.

Silence. Lyra whispered down:

'Sir, we must keep you hidden. I have a canvas bag – if that would be all right – I could carry you to our room …'

'Yes,' came the answering whisper from below.

Lyra pressed her ear to the trapdoor, and, hearing no more tumult, opened it carefully and then darted out to retrieve her bag and the books she'd been studying. The starlings had left evidence of their last meals on the covers of both books, and Lyra made a face as she thought about explaining it to the Librarian of St Sophia's. She picked the books up gingerly and took them and the bag down through the trapdoor, to hear Pan whispering, 'Sssh …'

Voices beyond the lower door: two men leaving Dr Polstead's room. Visitors – the university term hadn't yet begun, and he wouldn't be holding tutorials yet.

Lyra held open her bag. The strange dæmon hesitated. He was a witch's dæmon, and he was used to the wide Arctic skies. The narrow canvas

darkness was frightening to him.

'Sir, it will only be for five minutes,' she whispered. 'We can't let anyone else see you.'

'You are Lyra Silvertongue?'

'Yes, I am.'

'Very well,' he said, and delicately stepped into the bag that Lyra held open for him.

She picked it up carefully, waiting for the visitors' voices to recede down the stairs. When they'd gone, she stepped over Pan and opened the door quietly. Pan flowed through like dark water, and Lyra set the bag gently over her shoulder and followed, shutting the door behind her.

'Lyra? What's going on?'

The voice from the doorway behind her made her heart leap. Pan, a step ahead, hissed quietly.

'Dr Polstead,' she said, turning. 'Did you hear the birds?'

'Was that what it was? I heard a lot of banging,' he said.

He was stout, ginger-haired, affable; more inclined to be friendly to Lyra than she was to return the feeling. But she was always polite.

~~"You are an advocate for ... said~~
~~Emma laughing, tho' I do not exactly understand it."~~
~~Lord Osborne laughed rather awkwardly, & then said~~
~~"Upon my word, I am a bad one for compliments."~~
~~[illegible]~~
~~and after some minutes silence added, "Can you~~
~~give me a hint ... without offering~~
~~compt? I should be very glad to learn." Emma~~
~~could not say a syllable, & ... [illegible]~~
~~[illegible]~~
~~He had too much sense not to take the hint —~~
~~& when he spoke again, it was with a degree~~
~~of [illegible]~~
~~before [illegible] employing [illegible]~~
by a gracious answer, & a more full view
of her face than she had yet bestowed. ~~[illegible]~~
Unused to exert himself, & happy in contem:
:plating her, he sat in silence for some
minutes longer, while Tom Musgrave was chatter:
:ing to Elizth, till they were interrupted by Nanny's
[illegible] half [illegible] the door & putting

5

LESS IS MORE

Sasha Murphy

20/8/35

[illegible]

[illegible]

In architecture the motto 'Less is more' is linked to Mies van der Rohe. In literature it is often associated with Samuel Beckett, who saw his work in terms of 'lessness', in contrast with one of his most important literary fathers, James Joyce. Beckett knew what he was talking about, for in the late 1930s he had helped Joyce with the proofs of *Finnegans Wake*. Even at such a late stage in the writing process, Joyce 'was always adding to it', Beckett once said.[56] For Beckett, Joyce's accretive approach was connected to an encyclopaedic attempt at 'knowing more, [being] in control of one's material', whereas he himself realized that his own way was in 'impoverishment, in lack of knowledge and in taking away, in subtracting rather than in adding'.[57] This 'less is more' idea may have become a bit of a cliché, but it remains a powerful statement in the context of twentieth-century Western society, whose economy was basically driven by the more banal motto 'more more more'. At the beginning of the twenty-first century, in *Something New Under the Sun* (2001), the historian John McNeill gave a historical account of how unusual the twentieth century had been 'for the intensity of change and the centrality of human effort in provoking it'.[58] We have probably used ten times more energy in the last century than our ancestors used in the previous millennium. As a species we have become so numerous in the past century that we now collectively qualify as a geological force. For instance, the rate at which mammal species became extinct in the twentieth century was about forty times higher than 'normal'. We have refashioned the biosphere to an unprecedented degree. This phenomenon is 'something new under the sun'.

39 Opening page of Samuel Beckett's manuscript of the novel *Murphy*, dated 8 August 1935, with the opening sentence 'The sun shone as only the sun can, on nothing new.' (University of Reading UoR MS 5517/1, fol. 1r)

40 Doodles (including a drawing of James Joyce, with his eye patch) in the manuscript of Samuel Beckett's *Murphy* (University of Reading UoR MS 5517/1, fols 08v–09r)

41 The page of Samuel Beckett's manuscript of *Murphy* where the opening sentence takes its definitive shape: 'The sun shone, ~~it had~~ having no alternative, on the nothing new.' (University of Reading UoR MS 5517/1, fol. 10r)

~~Our sun shone, as ... on the nothing new, as its ... & their ..., as ... almost.~~

~~Our sun shone, as now alone can, on the nothing new.~~ ~~... nothing new.~~

5/9/35

Chapter 1. ~~Introducing~~ Murphy

~~M. is a man,~~

The sun shone, having no alternative, on the nothing new. Murphy sat out of it, being put down for one of the groves that abound in World's End London. Here, for what might have been a year, he had eaten, drunk, slept, & put his clothes on & off, in a medium-sized room of N.W. aspect commanding an unintercepted view of medium-sized rooms of S.E. aspect. Soon he would have to make other arrangements, because the premises had been condemned. Soon he would have to buckle to and start eating, drink, sleep, & put his clothes off & on, in

'the nothing new'

Against this background, it seems remarkable and almost provocatively defeatist that, in the first half of that same twentieth century, Samuel Beckett opened his first published novel *Murphy* (1938) with a reference to the Bible, according to which 'there is nothing new under the sun' (Ecclesiastes 1:9). Beckett's opening sentence reads:

> The sun shone, having no alternative,
> on the nothing new.[59]

It is worthwhile taking a closer look at the way this sentence was written. For in the manuscript it took Beckett almost ten attempts to arrive at the published version. He started writing his draft on 20 August 1935 (see fig. 39). The first two versions read:

> The sun shone as only the sun can, on nothing new.[60]

In the third version he changed 'as only the sun can' into 'as only suns can' – acknowledging the existence of other solar systems.

In the subsequent versions the variants are relatively small: 'The sun' changes into 'Our sun' (version 4); 'on nothing new' into 'on the nothing new' (version 5); 'as only suns can' into 'as only suns must' and then into 'as only a sun must' (version 6); 'as only suns can' into 'as suns alone can' (version 7). Day after day, Beckett keeps tinkering, producing variations on the theme, and he keeps crossing out whatever he writes.

Still, he does not give up, and even though the writing does not go well he stays on the page by drawing doodles. Usually, Beckett writes on the right-hand page only, using the left-hand page for additions, loose jottings or doodles. It is not only Charlie Chaplin who seems to have been on his mind,[61] but also James Joyce, as he draws his portrait with the characteristic eye patch – the man who kept adding, even at proof stage (see fig. 40).

The struggle to get the opening sentence right goes on until, on 5 September, in version 10 of the opening sentence, Beckett makes a change that has a more significant impact on the content. This version reads: 'The sun shone, ~~it had~~ having no alternative, on the nothing new' (10r; fig. 41).

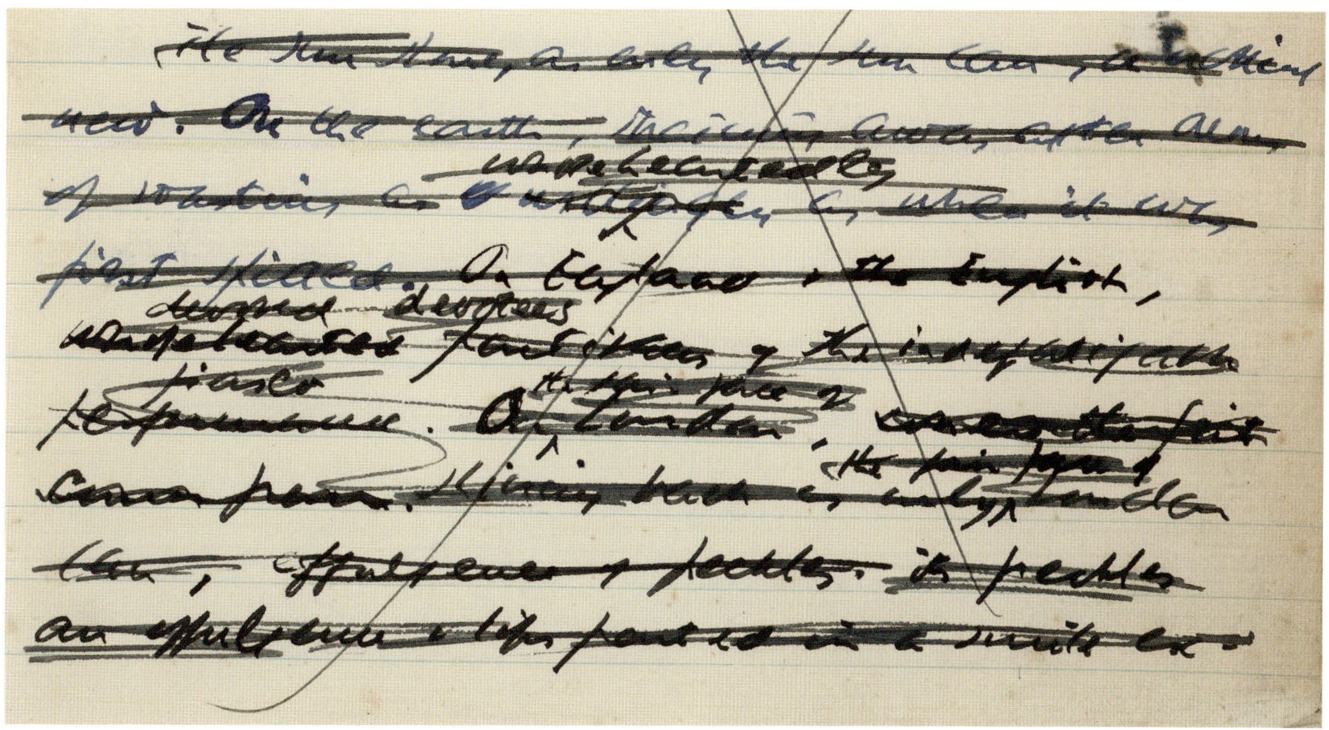

From this moment onwards, the writing suddenly seems to have proceeded more easily. By that time, it had taken Beckett more than two weeks (from 20 August to 5 September 1935) to write this one sentence.

Why is version 10 so fundamentally different? The early attempts all stress the fact that shining on the nothing new is something 'only the sun' or 'only suns' can do. The breakthrough moment comes down to a change of mindset, a mental shift: from shining as being something only the sun can do, to shining being the only thing the sun can do. After repeating day after day that only the sun can shine the way it does, suddenly this shining is presented as the only thing it can do. Among the many deletions, the shift is barely noticeable, but it arguably constitutes the most concise critique of the Enlightenment project. Although the early beginnings of the Enlightenment coincide, thanks to Copernicus and Galileo, with humanity's astronomical realization that 'its' earth is not the centre of the universe, humankind just seems to have psychologically dealt with this blow by means of a heliocentric reaction, acting (for centuries) as if it were the sun itself, letting everything turn around its shining self.

42 Detail of a cut passage in Samuel Beckett's manuscript of *Murphy* (University of Reading UoR MS 5517/1, 01r)

Starting a novel and fighting the fear of the blank page can be notoriously difficult. But even the story of Beckett's two-week battle for the opening sentence of *Murphy* is a reduction of the complexity that marked this process. For we have conveniently left out all kinds of side streets and roads not taken. The first version of the sentence, for instance, actually continues, specifying that the sun was shining, 'for example … on the earth, spitted on its axis, straining away after aeons of roasting, ~~as confidently~~ ~~hopefully.~~ no wiser than as when it was first spitted'.

This never made it to the final version. But Beckett did develop it in the second version, where the spitted earth is straining away 'willingly' and 'wholeheartedly', and the sun is also shining more specifically on England and the English, 'wholehearted partisans' and 'devotees of the indefatigable ~~performance~~ fiasco' (SEE FIG. 42).

This is Beckett the critic of the Enlightenment project in full force. One year later, he read *Faust* and noted down Goethe's lines on the human being's impulse to urge upwards and onwards ('Doch ist es jedem eingeboren, / dass sein Gefühl hinauf u. vorwärts dringt'[62]). In a letter to Thomas MacGreevy, Beckett referred to this *perpetuum mobile* as 'keep on keeping on', which he said he could understand only 'as a social prophylactic'.[63] He also excerpted a long passage from the introduction to the *Faust* edition by the editor Robert Petsch, about the thirst for action and Goethe's idea of the meaning of life, 'Tätigsein, Tüchtigsein, Vorwärtsstreben' (being active, proficient, striving forward), which basically comes down to the tautological cycle of going on to keep on going, and not being led into what the editor calls the 'temptation of stillness'.[64] Beckett's protagonist, Murphy, turns this around and actively strives for 'stillness', focusing on the little world, as opposed to the big world of quid pro quo, the world of capitalist logic and the necessity of economic growth, the world of 'meliorism', the belief that the world can be made better by human effort. Around this time, Beckett considered the alternative, not *vorwärts* but 'worstward': instead of 'meliorism' he coined the term 'pejorism', the belief that the world can be – and is being – made worse by all this human effort, by all this 'straining away', as it is called in the first versions of the opening sentence of *Murphy*: here, the sun is presented as 'an example of tireless endeavour of tenacity which … the great majority of its denizens has not ceased to follow'. He calls these self-declared enlightened human beings 'bugs of

Sisyphus' (a genus of dung beetles that make balls of droppings and roll them over the soil, not unlike the way Sisyphus rolled his rock up the hill according to Greek mythology): 'The bugs of Sisyphus think themselves big.' – Big as in the big world – 'Bloody bugs of Sisyphus.'

And the second version of the sentence describes how London imitates the sun, 'shining back as only the fair face of London can …, its freckles an effulgence', believing itself to be the centre of the universe. In the manuscripts, Beckett has crossed out all this shining effulgence, brightness and radiance, covering it with black ink.

Having brought the novel to a close in July 1936, Beckett's attention turned to finding a suitable publisher for *Murphy*, only to be confronted with requests to make it 'less' rather than 'more'. The publishing house Houghton Mifflin, for example, asked for the book to be shortened. In a letter to his friend and literary agent, George Reavey, Beckett expressed his dismay at this request:

> Let me say at once that I do not see how the book can be cut without being disorganised. Especially if the beginning is cut (& God knows the first half is plain sailing enough) the later part will lose such resonance as it has. I can't imagine what they want me to take out. I refuse to touch the section entitled Amor Intellectualis quo M. se ipsum amat. And I refuse also to touch the game of chess. The Horoscope chapter is also essential. But I am anxious for the book to be published and therefore cannot afford to reply with a blank refusal to cut anything. … Will you therefore communicate to Mr Greenslet my extreme aversion to removing one third of my work, proceeding from my extreme inability to understand how this can be done and leave a remainder.[65]

Beckett's letter gives voice to the dilemma faced by many young writers. On the one hand there is the desire to retain artistic control over one's work, and on the other the simple desire, or even practical necessity, of getting published. It is also a reminder of the influence exerted by editors. The necessary balancing act performed by authors is humorously expressed in Beckett's subsequent letter to George Reavey of 20 December 1936, in which he writes that 'The last I remember is my readiness to cut down the work to its title. I am now prepared to go further, and change the title, if it gives offence.'[66] In the event, Beckett had to wait another eighteen months before Routledge accepted the novel for publication, luckily without requesting any cuts.

'better abort than be barren'

The tension between the private and the public worlds of literary texts is also exemplified by a poem Beckett wrote immediately after finishing the novel *Murphy* in July 1936. The poem in question, titled 'Cascando', was first published in the October–December 1936 issue of the *Dublin Magazine*, and opens with the line 'is it not better abort than be barren'. The poem thus thematizes the threat of writer's block, of favouring abandonment over never putting pen to paper. Yet this opening sentence was originally preceded by the following two lines:

> why were you not simply what I despaired for
> an occasion of wordshed

Once again, an editor, this time Seamus O'Sullivan of the *Dublin Magazine*, asked for cuts, specifically to 'make one line of two somewhere, anywhere, in the interests of his pagination'.[67] As a result, Beckett cut the opening two lines, or, to use his words, the poem was 'Circumcised accordingly, it now begins with the abortion dilemma'.[68] The use of the word 'circumcised' here not only highlights the act of 'cutting away', but also speaks to the poem's themes of reproduction and (sexual) love. Indeed, when he received his copy of the *Dublin Magazine* while travelling through Germany in October 1936, Becket returned to the word, telling MacGreevy that, 'To judge by quantity of spare space that follows it, the circumcision was uncalled for.'[69]

Beckett's dismay at realizing that there had been no need to 'circumcise' his poem for publication follows on from what had been a fairly tortuous writing process. Indeed, while 'Cascando' was printed as a single poem in the *Dublin Magazine*, so far as Beckett was concerned he was actually submitting two poems, numbered '1' and '2', to O'Sullivan, without any title (the title and the third part, made up of only one line – 'Unless they love you' – were only added later). Beckett appears to have reflected on his struggle with 'Cascando' in an entry found in his 'Whoroscope Notebook': 'Cascando: praesectum decies ad unciam !!'.[70] The line, which translates as 'pruned down by a tenth to an ounce', is an adaptation of line 294 in Horace's *The Art of Poetry*: 'praesectum decies non castigavit ad unguem'. In the relevant passage Horace notes that a poem that has been chiselled ten times to perfect accuracy by time and revision should not be rejected. Judging by the position of the quotation in

43 Samuel Beckett's manuscript of 'Human Wishes' (University of Reading UoR MS 3458, fol. 03r)

(rising)

Mrs D. That is all the language of a gentlewoman, Miss Carmichael.

Miss C. (rising) I have all the advantages, Madam, of being the relict of a [illegible] master.

Mrs D. Be seated; and see

Mrs Williams. [illegible] the [illegible] [illegible] of your [illegible] polite society.

Miss Carmichael. Nor the daughter of a Welsh mechanic.

Mrs D. And whom you are the relict, the nameless relict, Miss Carmichael, of a low man. [illegible] to enquire.

Mrs W. I am most loath, madam, to [illegible] your syntax, [illegible] add: or of whom the progeny, of a low man.

Miss Carmichael: (Laughs heartily, & its [illegible] her room.)

on an earlier occasion, together with the Ethics of Geulincx, when I was given me at 7, 13 or 14. ~~He was the tutor~~ ~~to~~ They were a very fine pair of pince-nez, with gold branches. He was a far-seeing man. He was found ~~one~~ one morning, on the floor in his W.C., his dress in shocking disorder, ~~[illegible]~~ dead of an infarct.

Et on me sortait donc, entre autres choses, que je me couvrisse le bas du visage d'un drap noir et le demander l'aumône à un coin ensoleillé. Car il me semblait que mes yeux ~~[illegible]~~ n'étaient pas complètement éteints, grâce peut-être aux, comment dire, aux lunettes, ~~[illegible]~~ noires que mon tuteur m'avait données quand j'étais petit. Il m'avait donné, à la même occasion, l'Éthique de Geulincx. C'était une vieille paire de lunettes, ~~[illegible]~~ des ~~[illegible]~~ lunettes ~~[illegible]~~ d'homme avec la monture en or. C'était un homme prévoyant. On l'a trouvé mort, un matin, sur le plancher de ses W.C., les vêtements dans un désordre terrible, ~~[illegible]~~ foudroyé par un infarctus. L'Éthique portait son nom sur la page de garde et ~~[illegible]~~ les lunettes lui avaient peut-être appartenu aussi. Ce pont était maintenant

the notebook, Beckett probably wrote the line shortly before his arrival in Germany in early October 1936, where he would spend the next six months. If Beckett equated the poem's writing with such an exercise in revision, then the title 'Cascando', deriving from an Italian term, implies an act of falling, or in musical terms a decrease of volume and tempo, similar to 'decrescendo'. Indeed, Beckett strengthened the musical connection by choosing the word 'Mancando' for the title of his German translation of the poem, a direction for music to become softer, to die away.

The cluster of references employed by Beckett, both within the poem itself and to describe the writing of the poem, all circle around notions of refining and cutting. As Beckett struggled to write in the years leading up to the Second World War, the question of whether to stay silent or at least begin and then abort continued to be a vexed one. Indeed, while he was in Dresden during his tour of Nazi Germany from October 1936 to April 1937, he started a poem but only managed to put down two lines. As he noted in his diary: 'Have the mood for the first time since Farley episode, but spit in its eye .... Another little suicide.'[71] Beckett is here remembering the 'occasion of wordshed' that led to the composition of the poem 'Cascando', a brief love affair with a woman called Betty Stockton Farley, which was – because she was ultimately not interested in its continuation – quickly ended.

As it turned out, there would be many textual 'abortions' and 'suicides' over the next few years. Immediately after his return from his journey through Germany in April 1937, Beckett embarked on what would have been his first theatrical play. In order to prepare for the writing of 'Human Wishes', Beckett filled three notebooks with information about the life and work of the eighteenth-century writer Samuel Johnson. In the event, however, Beckett only managed to write one act of the play, in 1940, before abandoning it. Part of his problem was the fact that he had amassed too much material and could not find a way to distil it within a dramatic structure. Once again, Beckett doodled extensively in his manuscript in order to keep himself immersed in the compositional process (SEE FIG. 43). Here the text ends up being cut and replaced by visual metaphors and illustrations.

After the Second World War, another mode of 'cutting' comes into play as Beckett began to write in both English and French. On 17 February 1946 he started to write a short story in English entitled 'Suite' (as noted on the front cover of the notebook). On page 28, however, for reasons that remain unclear,

44 Samuel Beckett's manuscript of 'Suite' (the original title of the story 'La Fin'/'The End'), with the horizontal line marking a switch from English to French (Burns Library, Boston College, Beckett collection, Box 11, Folder 9, fol. 28r)

Beckett cut himself short, drawing a black horizontal line across the page (SEE FIG. 44).

When he continued writing, he did so in French, reworking the existing text and completing it three months later. But a more drastic cut was yet to come. Even before he had finished it, the story was accepted for publication in the French existentialist journal *Les Temps modernes*. However, having sent the first part of 'Suite' to the editors of the journal, he was subsequently informed by Simone de Beauvoir that the second part had been rejected. As such, only half of the story was published in the July 1946 issue of *Les Temps modernes*. The complete story, with the title 'La Fin', was only published in 1955, with the English version 'The End' following thereafter. Despite its title, 'The End' opened up the path for the 'suite' of Beckett's French writings, made possible by a horizontal line that marks a cut between two languages.

Beckett continued writing in French at an impressive pace. The writing seems to have been so easy that the first few years after the Second World War are generally considered the most creative period of his career. He wrote four novels, four stories, two plays and a dozen poems in five years. Apparently, switching to writing in French was for Beckett a key to successful composition. But the key to that 'success' was actually *de*composition. More than a century earlier, William Wordsworth famously defined 'successful composition', especially of poetry, not just as the spontaneous overflow of powerful feelings, but as a process of emotion recollected in tranquillity, and contemplated until an emotion kindred to the original one is gradually produced. Beckett is one of the first writers who most consistently questions this fixation on success and goes instead in the opposite direction.

The art of decomposition

In his novel *Molloy* (originally written in French), the eponymous character says: 'It is in the tranquillity of decomposition that I remember the long confused emotion which was my life.'[72] The way Beckett 'decomposed' his character involved all kinds of cutting, discarding, deleting, omitting, crossing out and revising. But the most remarkable thing is that he often did not cover up the traces of this decomposition. Instead, he deliberately left 'textual scars'. These scars draw the reader's attention to the process of cutting that preceded the published version of the text.

45 Printer's copy of Samuel Beckett's novel *Molloy* (University of Reading UoR MS 5859, page 214)

Ballyba. Les pâturages, malgré les pluies torrentielles, étaient d'une grande pauvreté et parsemés de rochers. N'y poussaient dru que le chiendent et une étrange graminée bleue et amère impropre à l'alimentation du gros bétail mais dont s'accommodaient tant bien que mal l'âne, la chèvre et le mouton noir. D'où Ballyba tirait-il donc ~~xxxxxxx sa richesse~~ son opulence. Je vais vous le dire. Non, je ne dirai rien. Rien. ~~Des selles de ses habitants. Et cela depuis les temps immémoriaux.~~ Quelques mots à ce sujet. C'est sans doute la dernière fois que j'aurais l'occasion de m'abandonner à ma passion pour la chose régionale, pour cette unique mixture qui donne à chaque terroir son bouquet, pour ce que j'appelle le folklore du sous-sol.

Bally était entouré de toutes parts d'une zone maraîchère large d'un demi-mille à peu près. Les primeurs les plus rares y voisinaient, dans ~~avec~~ une luxuriance effrénée, avec les racines de consommation courante tels le navet et la rave. Chaque année des centaines, que dis-je, des centaines de milliers de légumes impeccables de toutes sortes quittaient Ballyba à destination des marchés nationaux et étrangers, dans des tombereaux. Comment arrivait-on à cet agréable résultat? Grâce aux excréments des citoyens. Je m'explique.

Chaque personne pouvant être considérée, d'après le recensement le plus récent, comme ayant domicile dans Ballyba, et à partir de l'âge de deux ans, devait à l'O.M.B. (Organisation Maraîchère de Ballyba) tant de matières par an, à livrer mensuellement. Les quantités

A good example is the description of the Molloy country by the character Moran. While the first part of the novel is narrated by Molloy, Moran is the narrator of the second part. Before he sets out to look for Molloy, he describes the Molloy country, called 'Ballyba'. He talks about its geography and its agriculture, mentioning details such as 'a curious bitter blue grass fatal to cows and horses, though tolerated by the ass, the goat and the black sheep. And then he starts explaining Ballyba's economy:

> D'où Ballyba tirait-il donc ses richesses? Je vais vous le dire.
> What then was the source of Ballyba's prosperity? I'll tell you.[73]

In the manuscript, this is followed by a long description of Ballyba's remarkable economy, entirely based on the excrements of its citizens. According to Moran's account, the citizens' stools were the source of Ballyba's riches. Starting from the age of two, every citizen was to oblige the Market Gardening Organisation with a certain amount of faecal matter every year. To keep the faecal production at the highest level and producing primarily for the home market, travel abroad is strictly limited by the Organisation, headed by the Obidil (an anagrammatic mirror image of Libido), an official who is entirely dressed in white and who is the only one who can issue travel orders. The description is meticulous in the scatological details concerning this economy and can be read as a satire of Ireland's policy of economic protectionism in the 1930s, introduced by the Fianna Fáil government under Éamon de Valera.

When Beckett had finished a typescript of his novel and had shown it to confidants such as Mania Péron, he decided to cut the ten-page satirical passage (SEE FIG. 45). In the typescript submitted to the publisher, he crosses out the passage with a blue pencil, starting just after the sentence 'je vais vous le dire', adding above the line: 'Non, je ne dirai rien. Rien.' 'No, I'll tell you nothing. Nothing.'

If Beckett had simply wanted to omit this ten-page passage, he probably would have started the cut after the curious bitter blue grass, just before the question 'What then was the source of Ballyba's prosperity?' But he chose to let the narrator ask the question, say he was going to tell us, and then unsay his statement, according to a rhetorical device that Beckett was to develop in his subsequent novels: epanorthosis, or self-correction (for instance: They came with an army of 1,000, no – 10,000 soldiers!). Usually, this figure of speech is employed to add emphasis. Beckett, however, uses it primarily to draw attention to the act of self-correcting itself as a major, but often neglected, element in the way we write and think, composing a sentence, reconsidering, revising it on second thought, reconsidering again, revising again. Each revision implies a form of decomposition of the previous version.

As we saw in Chapter 1, a visually striking example of the way decomposition constitutes an inherent part of composition is the opening page of the first draft of Beckett's *Not I*, a play for just a mouth. Only the lips of the female protagonist are visible on stage. They give birth to the text, which actually starts with the word 'birth': 'birth into ~~the~~ this world … this world … of a ~~small~~ tiny baby ~~boy or girl~~ in a small … what? … girl?'.[74] This 'birth' remained the opening in at least four subsequent typescript versions until, in the fifth typescript, Beckett replaced it with 'out': '~~birth~~ out … into this world … this … world … tiny little thing'.[75]

Beckett thus kept polishing his text until it actually became rougher: from a baby's birth to a little 'thing' that is pushed 'out' prematurely ('before its time') – which comes closer to Beckett's typically self-deprecatory attitude towards his own creations. The curtness of the word 'out', emphasizing the severing of the infant from its mother's body, applies also to the text itself. By the act of writing it down, the thought is severed from its author's mind. The metaphor of giving birth to a literary text has a long tradition, but Beckett presents it in such a way that it recalls, if not the notion of an abortion, at least that of something cut short: 'out … into this world … this world … tiny little thing … before its time'. This may sound harsh, but when applied to the birth of the text itself, this sense of being premature is almost universally relevant to any first draft. It usually takes several weeks, months, sometimes years of mindful care to let it develop into a publication.

Of course, in Beckett's world 'birth' is always also the start of a process of dying. 'Birth was the death of him' is the first line of another late play, titled *A Piece of Monologue*, written in the 1970s. Around the same time, Beckett wrote a series of very short, doggerel-like poems, such as:

> there
> the life late led
> down there
> all done unsaid[76]

Here, the notion of 'epanorthosis' or self-correction becomes existential in the sense that life is presented as the attempt to undo what has been done at

46 Samuel Beckett's manuscript of the poem 'mots survivants', from *mirlitonnades* (University of Reading UoR MS 2460, fols 7v–8r)

birth. One has been put into the world and death sets in. The end is not when everything is said and done, but when it is unsaid. Still, for something to be unsaid, it needs first to be said. In the drafts of this poem, the opening 'there' was crossed out and Beckett considered replacing it with the line 'where / where but there'.[77] In the end, he decided to just go with 'there'. But the brief moment of indecision, when he crossed out the word 'there', pinpoints the rationale behind the exhibition 'Write Cut Rewrite': the word 'there' is crossed out, and yet it is still there nonetheless, as a cancelled inscription on the page. Beckett's work constantly draws attention – both on a textual and on an existential level – to all the things we cancel, annul, revoke, set aside, throw away.

He also does this in a very material manner. Most of these short poems, called *mirlitonnades*, are written on scraps of paper or throwaway objects, such as a packet of cigarettes, an old envelope, or a piece torn from the packaging of a Johnny Walker whisky bottle (SEE FIG. 46). On the back of this torn-off lid, he wrote a poem in French, starting with the words 'finie / ou peu s'en faut / la

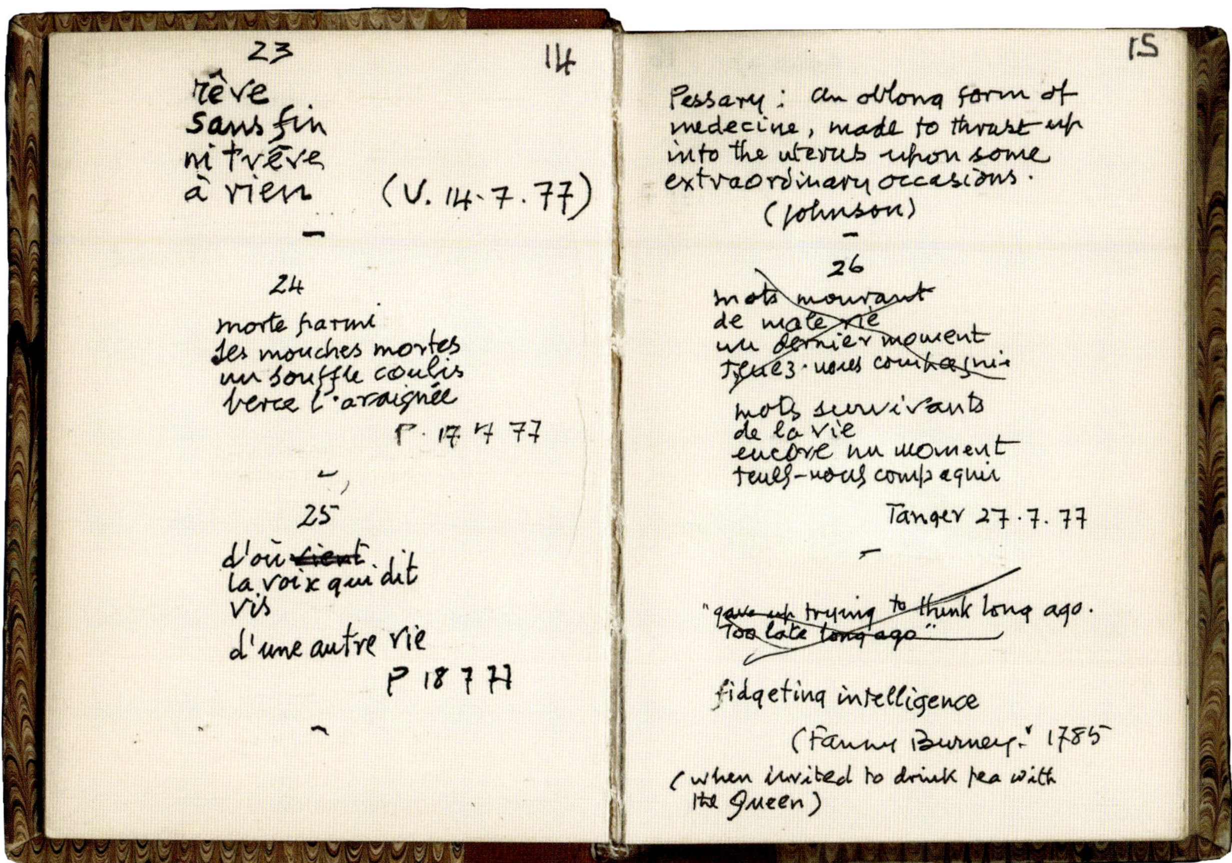
23 14

rêve
sans fin
ni trêve
à rien (V. 14.7.77)

—

24

morte parmi
les mouches mortes
un souffle coulis
berce l'araignée
P. 17 7 77

—

25

d'où ~~vient~~ dit
la voix qui dit
vis
d'une autre vie
P 18 7 77

—

15

Pessary: an oblong form of medecine, made to thrust up into the uterus upon some extraordinary occasions.
(Johnson)

—

26

~~mots mourant~~
~~de male vie~~
~~un dernier moment~~
~~tenez-nous compagnie~~

mots survivants
de la vie
encore un moment
tenez-nous compagnie

Tanger 27.7.77

—

"~~gave up trying to think long ago.~~
~~Too late long ago~~"

fidgeting intelligence
(Fanny Burney.' 1785
(when invited to drink tea with the Queen)

vie' (life finished, nearly),[78] a variation on the opening line of the play *Endgame*: 'Finished, it's finished, nearly finished, it must be nearly finished.'[79] Beckett kept undoing his words and wrote half a dozen versions of this poem on this little scrap of cardboard. In version 6, the opening words have changed to 'mots mourant' (words dying).

At that moment (27 July 1977) Beckett seemed to have been satisfied with this version, at least satisfied enough to copy it into his 'Sottisier' notebook, in which he wrote the fair copies of his *mirlitonnades*. But as soon as he had copied it (version 7) he changed his mind again, crossed it out, and wrote version 8, opening with the words 'surviving words': 'mots survivants / de la vie / encore un moment / tenez-nous compagnie / Tanger 27.7.77' (SEE FIG. 47). In the process of unsaying over the course of a lifetime, the words that have managed to survive life keep him company for just another moment.

What is most remarkable, however, is that Beckett then copied this final version one last time, back onto the Black Label scrap, and drew a frame around it. He thus insisted on presenting the final fair copy among the vestiges,

47 Samuel Beckett's 'Sottisier' Notebook containing two versions of the poem 'mots survivants' (University of Reading UoR MS 2901, fol. 7r)

the debris, the cuts, the flotsam and jetsam of the creative process, and he did so on a piece of paper that was saved from the wastepaper basket. Whereas the movement from the scrap to the notebook suggested a shift from the not-quite-right words (in the drafts) to the right words (the fair copy), the reinscription of the final version onto the scrap among the drafts marks a poetical statement about a fundamental linguistic scepticism, questioning the very notion of the right word, 'le mot juste' as the French writer Gustave Flaubert called it.

In his very last work, written after a brief spell of aphasia, Beckett makes this constant search for the right word thematic. The text is an imaginary writing process of a single sentence, which the fictional writer never manages to finish (SEE FIG. 48).

The longest version of this unfinished sentence is: 'folly for to need to seem to glimpse afaint afar away over there' and then he asks himself 'what', 'what is the word', and that is what the poem ends with, in Beckett's own translation: 'what is the word'. Since this is Beckett's last work, his entire œuvre thus ends in the middle of a sentence. The text turns the composition process – including all its forms of decomposition, all the cuts and all the wrong turns – into poetry. For as Molloy said: 'To decompose is to live, too.'[80]

48 Typescript of Samuel Beckett's last work, 'what is the word' (University of Reading UoR MS 3506)

<u>what is the word</u>

folly -
folly for to -
for to -
what is the word -
folly from this -
all this -
folly from all this -
given -
folly given all this -
seeing -
folly seeing all this -
this -
what is the word -
this this -
this this here -
all this this here -
folly given all this -
seeing -
folly seeing all this this here -
for to -
what is the word -
see -
glimpse -
seem to glimpse -
need to seem to glimpse -
folly for to need to seem to glimpse -
what -
what is the word -
and where -
folly for to need to seem to glimpse what where -
where -
what is the word -
there -
over there -
away over there -
afar -
afar away over there -
afaint -
afaint afar away over there what -
what -
what is the word -
seeing all this -
all this this -
all this this here -
folly for to see what -
glimpse -
seem to glimpse -
need to seem to glimpse -
afaint afar away over there what -
folly for to need to seem to glimpse afaint afar away over there what -
what -
what is the word -

what is the word

~~"You owe me an explanation of your compliment my Lord," said Emma laughing, "tho' I do not exactly understand it."~~ [defiance]

~~Lord Osborne laughed rather awkwardly & then said~~

~~"Upon my word, I am a bad one for compliments.~~ ~~[illegible]~~

~~[illegible]~~

~~and after some minutes silence, added~~ ~~[illegible]~~

~~[illegible] without offering~~

~~Compt. [illegible] glad to [illegible]~~

~~[illegible] syllable [illegible]~~

~~[illegible]~~

~~[illegible] freedom of her manner~~

~~He had too much sense not to take the hint~~ —

~~& when he spoke again, it was with a degree of courtesy & propriety which he had never [employed] before. [illegible]~~

by a gracious answer, & a more [full] view of her face than she had yet bestowed. ~~[illegible]~~

Unused to exert himself, & happy in contemplating her, he [then] sat in silence for [some] ~~[illegible]~~ minutes longer, while Tom Musgrave was chattering to Eliz:th, till they were interrupted by Nanny's [half] [illegible] the door & putting

6

CENSORSHIP & SELF-CENSORSHIP

ESTRAGON (Contd.) Wouldn't it, Didi?

VLADIMIR Calm yourself.

ESTRAGON (Voluptuously) Calm...calm...The English say cawm. (Pause) You know the story of the Englishman in the brothel?

VLADIMIR Yes.

ESTRAGON Tell it to me.

VLADIMIR Ah stop it!

ESTRAGON An Englishman having drunk a little more than usual takes himself to a broth~l. The bawd asks him if he wants a fair one, a dark one or a red-haired one. Go on.

VLADIMIR STOP IT!

(Exit VLADIMIR hurriedly. ESTRAGON gets up and follows him as far as the limit of the stage. Gestures of ESTRAGON like those of a spectator encouraging a pugilist. Enter VLADIMIR, he brushes past Estragon, crosses the stage with bowed head. ESTRAGON takes a step towards him, halts)

ESTRAGON (Gently) You wanted to speak to me? (Silence. ESTRAGON takes a step forward) You had something to say to me? (Silence. Another step forward) Didi...

VLADIMIR (Without turning) I've nothing to say to you.

ESTRAGON (Step forward) You're angry? (Silence. Step forward) Forgive me. (Silence. Step forward. ESTRAGON lays his hand on Vladimir's shoulder) Come, Didi. (Silence) Give me your hand. (VLADIMIR turns) Embrace me! (VLADIMIR stiffens) Don't be stubborn. (VLADIMIR softens. They embrace. ESTRAGON recoils) You stink of garlic!

VLADIMIR It's good for the kidneys. (Silence. ESTRAGON looks attentively at the tree) What do we do now?

ESTRAGON We wait.

VLADIMIR Yes, but while we wait.

ESTRAGON What about hanging ourselves?

VLADIMIR Hmm. It'd give us an erection.

ESTRAGON (Highly excited) An erection!

VLADIMIR With all that ensues. Where it falls mandrakes grow. That's why they shriek when you tear them up. Did you not know that?

ESTRAGON Let's hang ourselves immediately.

VLADIMIR From a bough? (they go towards the tree) I wouldn't trust it.

ESTRAGON We can always try.

VLADIMIR Go ahead.

ESTRAGON After you.

VLADIMIR No no, you first.

ESTRAGON Why me?

VLADIMIR You're lighter than I am.

ESTRAGON Just so!

VLADIMIR I don't understand.

ESTRAGON Use your intelligence, can't you.

(VLADIMIR uses his intelligence)

VLADIMIR (Finally) I remain in the dark.

ESTRAGON This is how it is. (he reflects) The bough... the bough... (angrily) Use your head, can't you?

VLADIMIR You're my only hope.

ESTRAGON (With effort) Gogo light - bough not break - Gogo dead. Didi heavy - bough break - Didi alone. Whereas -

VLADIMIR I hadn't thought of that.

ESTRAGON If it hangs you it'll hang me.

VLADIMIR But am I heavier than you?

ESTRAGON So you tell me. I don't know. There's an even chance. Or nearly.

VLADIMIR Well? What do we do?

ESTRAGON Don't let's do anything. It's safer.

Arguably the most feared and maligned form of cutting in literature is censorship. Samuel Beckett was confronted with it many times in his career. One of the famous cases is the first edition of *Waiting for Godot*. In Great Britain the Lord Chamberlain had been appointed as the censor of theatrical performances in 1737. The so-called Licensing Act gave him the power to prevent any performance from being staged, and to prosecute theatre owners for staging anything that had not received his approval. Not until the Theatres Act of 1968 was the Lord Chamberlain's authority to censor plays repealed. But that was too late for *Waiting for Godot*. Beckett had written the play in French (*En attendant Godot*) and the premiere had taken place in Paris on 4 January 1953. On 7 September of that year he sent a copy of his first draft translation to the British actor-director Peter Glenville, who had taken a joint option on the play together with British producer and theatre executive Donald Albery to stage a production in England. On 23 March 1954 Albery therefore submitted a copy of the typescript for approval to the Lord Chamberlain's office. This copy is still preserved in the Lord Chamberlain Play Collection at the British Library (MS-BL-LCP-1954–23). It consists of 102 leaves and is bound in a green cover with a white label of the 'Lord Chamberlain's Office', indicating that this is item 'N° 6597', entitled 'Waiting for Godot', to be staged at the 'Criterion Theatre'. The 'Date of Licence' mentioned on the label is '1.7.54'. The considerable delay between the submission of the request and the acquisition of a licence was due to the fact that the Lord Chamberlain did not approve of the script.[81]

Beckett was not so well known at that time. When Albery submitted the manuscript, he had tried to emphasize the playwright's importance by mentioning in the cover letter that Beckett 'was at one time James

49 Typescript of Samuel Beckett's *Waiting for Godot*, submitted for approval to the Lord Chamberlain's Office on 23 March 1954 (British Library, Lord Chamberlain Play Collection MS-BL-LCP-1954–23, fol. 09r–10r)

Joyce's secretary'.[82] This may actually have had the opposite effect. Joyce's *Ulysses* had been banned in the UK when it was published in 1922 because of its perceived obscenity. Even though the ban had been lifted in 1936, the connection with Joyce appears to have prejudiced the Assistant Examiner, Mr Turnbridge, who compiled a report for his colleagues at the Lord Chamberlain's Office on 28 March 1954. Turnbridge describes Joyce as 'the Irish author who, finding it necessary to invent virtually a new language to express himself, left his message to the world far from clear in consequence.' And he immediately draws attention to a concrete passage: 'The Joyce influence and attitude will be seen by a glance at Act I, pp. 40–41' of *Waiting for Godot*, which is Lucky's monologue. As a result, Turnbridge offered to 'indicate for elimination the words and lines of Joycean grossness', which amounted to fourteen passages, all highlighted in fuchsia ink on the script (SEE FIG. 49).[83] The Assistant Examiner's accompanying comments are followed by the advice of two colleagues – who did not always agree – added in blue ink and grey pencil after each passage in the report.[84] For instance, at a certain point in the play, the two protagonists, Vladimir and Estragon, consider hanging themselves from the tree by which they are waiting for Godot:

> ESTRAGON What about hanging ourselves?
> VLADIMIR Hmm. It'd give us an erection.
> ESTRAGON (highly excited) An erection!
> VLADIMIR With all that ensues. Where it falls mandrakes grow. That's why they shriek when you tear them up. Did you not know that?
> ESTRAGON Let's hang ourselves immediately.[85]

The passage creates a strong tension between vitality and death, but the Lord Chamberlain's Office objected and marked it with a red (fuchsia) line in the margin. The comment in the report reads: 'The lines as marked about a known secondary effect of hanging must come out.' The two colleagues both agreed: 'Yes' / 'Cut'.

As a result, the first British edition (Faber & Faber, 1956) was expurgated and the passage read:

ESTRAGON What about hanging ourselves?
Vladimir whispers to Estragon
VLADIMIR With all that ensues. Where it falls mandrakes grow. That's why they shriek when you tear them up. Did you not know that?
ESTRAGON Let's hang ourselves immediately.[86]

The idea of letting Vladimir whisper in Estragon's ear was a makeshift solution, but it did not work onstage. The passage lost its tension, mainly because it was hardly possible for the audience to figure out what was being whispered. Luckily, an unexpurgated edition was published in 1965, which restored the original scene.

As to Lucky's speech, in which the Assistant Examiner had detected 'the Joyce influence and attitude', he commented: 'Mixed in the nonsense of the first 12 lines, I detect distinct mockery of religion'. His colleagues' opinions were divided: one said 'Cut', the other 'Allow'.

In the second act, to kill time while waiting, Vladimir suggests they could play, acting as if they were Pozzo and Lucky. Estragon plays Pozzo, Vladimir does Lucky. As part of this game, Vladimir instructs Estragon to curse him, and so he does, calling Vladimir 'Gonoccoccus! Spirochaete!' The Assistant Examiner objected, commenting: 'These are the microbes of gonorrhaea and syphilis', and his colleagues concurred: 'Cut' / 'Cut'. As Barbara Pym noted (see Chapter 1), 'a slight tendency towards eccentricity' may have been a qualification necessary to work in the censorship business. Beckett did not lose his sense of humour during the whole negotiation with the bigoted team of censors. When they presented him with the list of cuts, he suggested 'Gonoccoccus! Spirochaete!' be replaced by two other abusive terms: 'Lord Chamberlain! Civil Servant!'[87]

Still, when his next play, *Endgame*, came out in 1958, Beckett was adamant that it should be published as he wrote it, ignoring the Lord Chamberlain's suggested cuts. In 1957 he wrote to his London agent, Rosica Colin:

> I shall not authorize a bowdlerized edition. If I had known that Faber were going to bring out Godot in the Lord Chamberlain's text I should have refused my auth[orization]. But they did this without consulting me. If I can only be published in England in an expurgated form, I prefer not to be published at all.'[88]

This time the Lord Chamberlain's Office had not just predictably objected to words like 'pee', 'balls' and 'arses', but especially to the prayer scene. Hamm suggests to Clov and Nagg that they pray to God. They assume an attitude of prayer and wait in silence, but nobody seems to listen to their prayers – to which Hamm reacts with the exclamation: 'The bastard! He doesn't exist!'

This time, Beckett told the director, George Devine, that 'this does call for a firm stand': 'I am afraid I simply cannot accept omission or modification of the prayer passage which appears to me indispensable as it stands' (26 December 1957).[89] To Alan Schneider, the director of the first US production of *Endgame*, he was even fiercer: 'In London the Lord Chamberlain demands inter alia the removal of the entire prayer scene! I've told him to buckingham off.'[90]

As a result, the Lord Chamberlain could not grant a licence for the public performance of *Endgame*, which caused a public outcry in the London newspapers in February 1958. The negotiations had reached an impasse, but by early summer the 'Lord Chamberpot' – as Beckett now called him – started showing some goodwill, saying that they would allow the scene to stand if Beckett changed one word: 'bastard'. Beckett made a concession and suggested they change it into 'swine': 'The swine! He doesn't exist!' Curiously, that was fine with the Lord Chamberlain. When Beckett wrote to his American publisher, Barney Rosset, that the play was at last licensed for public performance because 'swine' had been accepted as a substitute for 'bastard', he concluded: 'Hope God is pleased.'[91]

Self-censorship

The fear of being censored often leads to self-censorship. The work of Stephen Spender (1909–1995) is a striking example. In the United Kingdom homosexual activity between men was illegal until the Sexual Offences Act of 1967. In the German Weimar Republic of the late 1920s the atmosphere was more liberal than in the UK. In 1929 Spender spent a memorable summer in Germany with a group of friends, including W.H. Auden, Christopher Isherwood and Herbert List. He wrote a semi-autobiographical novel about it, *The Temple*. The title, inspired by Christ speaking of 'the temple of his body',[92] implicitly alludes to the descriptions of homosexual encounters in the novel, which was published only in 1988, more than fifty years after it was written. In that half century,

Spender rewrote the book several times, often applying forms of self-censorship in an attempt to circumvent the legal restrictions.

Spender presented his manuscript to various friends, including Auden and Isherwood, for their feedback.[93] He also sent it to the publisher Faber & Faber in 1931, but Geoffrey Faber 'considered the manuscript unpublishable', considering it 'both libellous and pornographic'.[94] In 1962 – five years before the 1967 Sexual Offences Act – Spender sold it to the Harry Ransom Center in Texas. That might have been the end of it: the novel would have been buried in the archive, unpublished and hidden from the public because some of the activities described in it were illegal in the UK. But in 1986 Spender's friend John Fuller found it in the archive and reminded Spender of it. According to the author, he then 'wrote at once to the librarian for a xerox of this'.[95] Two years later it was published by the same publisher that felt they had to refuse it half a century earlier.

The original manuscript ('FOR W.H. AUDEN') is still at the Harry Ransom Center, and the 'xerox' which Spender asked for in 1986 is preserved at the Bodleian Library in Oxford, with green and black ink deletions and additions in Spender's hand (SEE FIG. 50). This version opens with a passage that presents itself as a fragment 'From my Journal'.

This opening corresponds with the first typescript (dedicated 'To W.H. AUDEN & TONY HYNDMAN'):

> 1929 July 22nd. (Hamburg)
>
> Now I shall begin to live.
>
> Resolutions for the Long Vac. To do absolutely none of the work set for me by my Oxford tutor. Now I am away from England I shall begin my own work, and, whether I stay at Oxford or not, from now on, I shall continue to do that and no work but that.
>
> My own work is to write poetry and novels. I have no character or will-power outside my work. In the life of action, I do everything that my friends tell me to do, and have no opinions of my own. This is shameful, I know, but it is so. Therefore I must develop that side of me which is independent of other people. I must live and mature in my writings. My aim is to achieve maturity of soul.
>
> I shall now begin to keep a journal. This will contain descriptive notes of my surroundings, of people, of dialogue etc. …
>
> After my work, all I live for is my friends.
>
> Now to begin my journal.
>
> How did I get here?

OVERLEAF

50 Xeroxed manuscript of Stephen Spender's *The Temple* (Oxford, Bodleian Library, MS. Spender 330, p. 1)

51 Corrected printout of Stephen Spender's *The Temple*, in which the first person is changed to 'Paul' (Oxford, Bodleian Library, MS. Spender 312, p. 2)

The Temple.

From my Notebook Journal.

1929. July 22nd. (Hamburg)

Now I shall begin to live.

Resolutions for the Long Vac. To do absolutely none of the work set for me by my Oxford tutor. Now I ~~sh~~ am away from England I shall begin my own work, and, whether I stay at Oxford or not, from now on, I shall continue to do that and no work but that.

My own work is to write poetry and novels. I have no character or will-power outside my work. In the life of action, I do everything that my friends tell me to do, and have no opinions of my own. This is shameful I know, but it is so. Therefore I must develope that side of me which is independent of other people. I must live and mature in my writings. My aim is to achieve maturity of soul.

I shall now begin to keep a journal. This will contain descriptive notes of my surroundings, of people, of dialogue etc. ~~[illegible] everything I write must be written in good English, not only my letters and [illegible], I shall try to exercise the same discipline over my style.~~

After my work, all I live for is my friends.

Now to begin my journal.

How did I get here?

Well, one day, ~~[illegible]~~ at lunch-time, I was standing in ~~the lodge of the college~~ Univ. Lodge, and I was wondering whether my friend Marston would pass through it on his way to lunch. ~~[illegible] the notice-boards in which~~, in order to pass time I was looking at the notice-boards, a young don stopped to talk to me. He was with a very ~~[illegible]~~ smart, quiet-looking young man, to whom he introduced me. The young man was a German from Hamburg

1.

THE STOCKMANN HOUSE

FROM PAUL SCHONER'S JOURNAL, 1929.

July 22. From Paul Schoner's Notebook

Now I shall begin to live.

Resolutions for the Oxford Vac:--

To do absolutely none of the work set for me by my Oxford tutor.

Now that I am away from England, I shall do my own work, and, whether I stay at Oxford or leave, from now on, I shall continue to do that and no work except that.

My own work is to write poetry and fiction. I have no character or will power outside my work. In the world of action I do everything my friends tell me to do. I have no opinions of my own. This is shameful I know, but it is so. Therefore I must develop that side of my life which is independent of others. I must live and mature in my writing. My aim is to achieve maturity of soul.

I shall now begin to keep a journal. This will contain descriptions of people, specimens of dialogue copied down from life.

After my work, all I live for is my friends.

Now to begin my journal.

How did I get to Hamburg?

Well, one day last term, just before lunch, I was standing in University College Lodge and wondering whether my friend (as I still think of him) Marston--with whom I had gone on a walking tour along the river

That is how the narrative is set in motion. The first-person narrator is waiting for a friend called Marston at the lodge of his college, when someone else, a 'very suave, quiet looking young man' from Hamburg, called Ernst Stockman, starts talking to him and eventually invites him to Hamburg. The 'I' does not have a name, but other characters refer to him as 'S.' (as in Stephen Spender).

The same character Ernst Stockman reappears in a new typescript version ('FOR CHRISTOPHER ISHERWOOD AND W.H. AUDEN'), also held at the Bodleian (MS. Spender 330, *c.* 1930–1933). Here, however, the type of narrator has changed dramatically. The first-person narration is turned into a third-person narration; and the male protagonist 'S.' has been replaced by 'Catherine Crawleigh':

> PART ONE.
>
> I
>
> HIS head was like the caged head of a vulture. Getting out of the train, Catherine saw it first thus, behind bars. The complexion was the horned yellow colour of a beak. The eyes were spectacled and bird-like with conceited, metallic stare, fixed and hard, sometimes closed, blinking, then hard again.
>
> She knew that this was Ernst Stockmann waiting to meet her. Turning her eyes away again, she concentrated on getting through the crowd to the ticket collector. In doing so, she lost sight of him, she was so jostled by porters and fellow-travellers. Her eyes saw different angles of black and pink rising and then collapsing, the hard colour and smell and contact of many people. It was not till she reached the barrier that she thought of Ernst again, and then the first vivid, photographic impression of him had been blotted from her memory, although it was to remain fixed in her mind, an image with which she was unconsciously to compare all her future impressions of him.
>
> 'Miss Catherine Crawleigh?' he asked, bowing, and smiling slightly, as they shook hands. Then he continued 'Perhaps, if you are going to stay with us for long, I cannot begin too soon just to call you "Catherine"?'

This gender shift also changes the focalization and ultimately the narrative to such a degree that – with hindsight – Spender considered it an 'absurdity'. In a journal entry of 8 December 1976, he notes:

> I found in the 'bottomless pit' where all our stuff is buried rather than stored, three typed volumes of a novel I wrote in – I surmise – 1931 (funny how one didn't date things in those days) called *The Temple*. With my hopeless inability to read things I've put aside, I hadn't read this for over thirty years and was astonished how evocative and alive it is. An absurdity is that I've made the main character – myself – a girl. This was doubtless out of fear of censorship.[96]

By that time, censorship had become a major theme in Spender's life. In 1968, responding to an open letter in *The Times* from the Soviet dissidents Larisa Bogoraz and Pavel Litvinov drawing attention to the persecution of writers in the USSR, Spender created a committee, called Writers and Scholars International. This led to the foundation in 1972 of the magazine Index of Censorship.

Ten years after he found his self-censored version of *The Temple* in his 'bottomless pit', Spender started revising the xerox he received from the Harry Ransom Center. The revision is a confrontation between the artist as a young man (1929) and his much older self (1986). Many of the revisions are cuts. For instance, the artist as an old man writes 'delete?' in the left margin next to a passage written by his younger self, describing how Ernst stands with his hands set on his hips to show off the muscles of his arms, and admitting that 'His nakedness, unlike that of the common people, did make me feel ashamed for him.'[97]

The whole manuscript was typed out again, starting with the Journal entry, but this time it is presented as an '(<u>Entry in Paul Schoners Journal on July 22 1929 the evening of his arrival at the Stockmann residence in Hamburg</u>)'. In other words, the protagonist's name was changed again – from 'S.' to 'Catherine' to 'Paul' (SEE FIG. 51).

The question that sets the narrative in motion is still the same in the typed layer: 'How did I get to Hamburg?' But then Spender reread the typescript and revised it with a black pen. The most notable change is that he replaces 'I' with 'Paul', throughout the typescript: 'How did Paul get to Hamburg?' (MS. Spender 312). On the title page he noted: 'The original manuscript was dedicated in 1930 to W.H. Auden and

Christopher Isherwood. Now I add: "With memories of Herbert List."' He made numerous changes and cuts, such as the passage on Marston on page 3, next to which he wrote in big capital letters: 'OMIT' (SEE FIG. 52). While the young writer felt the need to self-censor his novel by turning his alter ego into a girl, the author as an older man had the chance to undo this self-censorship.

52 Corrected printout of Stephen Spender's *The Temple*, with a long passage marked 'OMIT' in the left margin (Oxford, Bodleian Library, MS. Spender 312, p. 3)

Wye, during the Easter vacation, would pass through the Lodge on his way to eat in Hall. The walking tour had led to our deciding not to meet, although, I suppose, we remain friends. The reason why we agreed that we should not meet was that we agreed that I bored him. Marston is an athlete, though his real passion is solo flying. He wants to join the RAF. I idolized him because he seemed to me a person of peculiar innocence and purity, untouched by the vulgarity and violence of his fellow athletes, like someone who lives alone on an island--an ancient Greek island which is also very English. On our walk, in order to bore him I never talked about anything I was interested in but almost exclusively about aeroplanes and flying, about which I had read several books the week previously. I fussed him much more than I did over myself. Once when he had a slight stomach ache I imagined a most terrible pain and kept on casting anxious glances at him, to see whether he had it until he said "Please don't fuss over me like an old hen." At the beginning of the term I had a long talk with him in which I admitted that I liked him much too much for him to be anything but irritated and bored by me, and perhaps we should not meet. He listened with real interest and attention to everything I said, remarking at the end of it: "This is the only conversation I've ever had with you which hasn't bored me, old son": and it was with a kind of mutual recognition like a kiss that we agreed not to meet ("if that's what you really want, old son").

Although I avoided going into Hall if I thought he was going to be there it nevertheless made my day to see him pass through the lodge as he went in. As I lingered there, pretending to read college notices, the new young dean, Dr Lawd, appeared from the quadrangle and, seeing me standing there, stopped, saying what luck that he should have run into me, because he wanted me, the college poet, to meet his companion, a young German, Dr

freedom of his manner.

by a gracious answer, & a more liberal full view of her face than she had yet bestowed. Unused to exert himself, & happy in contemplating her, he then sat in silence for some minutes longer, while Tom Musgrave was chattering to Eliz:th, till they were interrupted by Nanny's half opening the door & putting

7

DIFFICULT BEGINNINGS, ALTERNATIVE ENDINGS

27th Sept 1971. (1)

I still see him there. At night or when my mind wanders during class, On winter afternoons ~~by~~ when ~~the mist~~ slides off the ~~Cairn~~ Quant hills into our valley, I see his fat shadow tucked into the tree trunks and his round face smiling ~~at me~~ in the gloom. He'd ~~had~~ too. ~~chosen~~ picked the right place, ~~of course he'd always had~~ ~~best~~ A good eye for territory & had Tarz, ~~better than I gave him credit for in those days I'll admit~~ though I didn't give him credit for it in those days. Those trees ~~closest of~~ are at ~~in~~ the South east corner ~~of the pitch~~, ~~in a~~ in a clump ~~clump~~ at the lowest point of the playing fields. In Summer there's an easy form to the ~~foot of them~~, ~~but~~ and in winter

THE OPENING OF A NOVEL often does not coincide with the beginning of its genesis. And once the opening scene comes into view, it can sometimes take months for the right opening sentence to crystallize. The two weeks it took Beckett to write the opening sentence of *Murphy* (see Chapter 5) are lightning speed compared to the months it took John le Carré (pseudonym of David John Moore Cornwell, 1931–2020) to write the opening scene of *Tinker Tailor Soldier Spy*, his novel about the discreet, self-effacing spymaster George Smiley's attempts to uncover a Soviet mole in the British Secret Intelligence Service ('the Circus'). Smiley is living in forced retirement due to a failed operation which resulted in the torture of agent Jim Prideaux. The novel opens with Jim, who after the failed operation now teaches at a boys' prep school. Jim is being watched by Ricki Tarr, a field agent who was trained by Smiley and who supplies information that suggests there is a Soviet mole in the Circus. It is worth following the slow development from the first drafts to the moment le Carré finds the opening sentence, to fully realize how much cutting is involved in writing, how hard the work of revising is, and how much persistence it takes.

Opening 'seen'

On 27 September 1971 le Carré starts off with a first-person narration: the narrator is Jim, and the scene is totally focused on the sense of sight (FIG. 53). Two spies, Jim and Tarr, are watching each other the way professional watchers do:

> I still see him there. At night or when my mind wanders during class, on winter afternoons when the mist slides off the ~~Cesse~~ Quantock hills into our valley, I see his fat shadow tucked into the tree trunks and his round face smiling ~~at me~~ in the gloom.

53 First draft of John le Carré's *Tinker Tailor Soldier Spy*, when the opening scene was about two spies, Jim and Tarr, watching each other, and started with 'I still see him there' (Oxford, Bodleian Library, MS. le Carré 23)

long grass that grows between them, in winter the rugger slips down that way, so that if you were a proud parent wanting to watch the game, all you had to do was stand roughly where Tarr stood, under the same elms, and let the slope bring it to you. Not, God knows, that Tarr was watching the game, though did he clap his hands a couple of times, and once I even heard him murmur 'well done, well done' very confidingly to a boy who had done nothing. Tarr was watching me, Jim boy, as he called me, Teacher of French and rugger to the sons of the rich. watching He obliquely, the way watchers watch one another,

Several were standing there now, in fact, a partial screen for him.

54 First draft of *Tinker Tailor Soldier Spy*, showing le Carré in doubt as to whether he is going to use the accusative 'me' or 'Jim' as the one whom Tarr is watching (Oxford, Bodleian Library, MS. le Carré 23)

55 First typescript of John le Carré's *Tinker Tailor Soldier Spy*, cutting the word 'there' in the original opening sentence (Oxford, Bodleian Library, MS. le Carré 23)

Sept. 27th. 71

I still see him. At night or when my mind wanders during class, on winter afternoons when the mist slides off the Quantock hills into our valley, I see his fat shadow tucked into the tree trunks and his round face smiling in the gloom. He'd picked the right day of course. Our first eleven was playing an away match and several of the senior staff including ~~Elmington~~ the headmaster had gone with them in the ~~coach~~ bus.

But the under elevens were playing Hazlegrove at home. As duty master it was my job to referee & take care of the camp followers at tea. So Tarr had it all his own way: a half empty school, the cover of a handful of strangers all thinking he belonged to someone else, and me stuck out in the middle of a field with thirty little boys to tie me down. As to the weather, he might have ordered it: mist, and a thin soaking rain that made curtains where it blew.

He'd picked the right place, too. A good eye for territory had Tarr, though I didn't give him credit for it in those days. Those trees are at the south east corner, ~~in~~ They stand in a clump at the lowest point of the playing field. In summer there's an easy four to the long grass that grows between them, and in winter the rugger slips down that way, so that if you were a proud parent wanting to watch the game, all you had to do was stand roughly where Tarr stood, under the same elms, and let the slope bring it to you. Not, God knows, that Tarr was watching the game, though he did clap his hands a

'~~at me~~' is cut because it is precisely not at Jim that Tarr is smiling; he is smiling at the boys playing rugby on the playing field to hide the fact that he is actually watching Jim. Further in the opening paragraph, when the watching game is made explicit (SEE FIG. 54), le Carré is in doubt as to whether he is going to use the accusative 'me' or 'Jim':

> ~~He~~ Tarr was watching ~~me~~ ~~Jim~~ me. Jim boy, as he called me, teacher of French and rugger to the sons of the rich. ~~Watching~~ Watching ~~me there~~ ~~Aged fifty and wearing x~~ ~~Obliquely~~ me obliquely, the way watchers watch one another

The very same day (SEE FIG. 55), it was typed out:

> I still see him ~~there~~.

One of the first things he cut was 'there', so that the attention is concentrated on just the watchers watching: 'Not, God knows, that Tarr was watching the game' (version 2; SEE FIG. 55).

This is where the third version – a typescript marked 'TINKER TAILOR' in big red capital letters, dated 28 September 1971 and missing its first page – picks up. The hesitation between 'me' and 'Jim' is still present:

> Not, God knows, that Tarr was watching the game … No, Tarr was watching ~~me~~ Jim. Jim boy, as he called me. Teacher of French and rugger to the sons of the rich. Watching me obliquely, the way watchers watch one another … I was watching Tarr, too and thinking: I won't go back, nothing on God's earth will make me go back, I'm fifty and out of the game.

The next two versions – dated 5 October and 15 October 1971 – keep the opening line 'I still see him', which creates a tension between the present (the moment of narration) and the past (the moment of experience): 'Tarr was watching Jim … I was watching Tarr'. This interesting moment of hesitation between 'me' and 'Jim' eventually led to a change from first-person to third-person narration. Le Carré decided not to start with 'I' anymore, but with a more traditional description (handwritten again) and Tarr instead of Jim as the perceiving agent (SEE FIG. 56):

56 New opening scene of John le Carré's *Tinker Tailor Soldier Spy*, starting with the sentence 'It was early December when Tarr called, afternoon, about three' (Oxford, Bodleian Library, MS. le Carré 24)

> It was early December when Tarr called, afternoon, about three. A fat yellow mist had that morning rolled down the bracken coombs of the Quantocks and covered the school, the playing fields and the redstone village. And though Tarr loathed this bad weather as another man might loathe ill health,

It was early December when Tarr called, afternoon, about three. A fat yellow mist had that morning rolled down the bracken coombs of the Quantocks and covered the school, the playing fields and the redstone village. And though Tarr loathed this bad weather as another man might loathe ill health, the hostility of that December dark suited him so well he might have ordered it. For he knew that bad weather makes strangers of us all; even the naturally curious forget to stare.

The school buildings, as Tarr moved quietly across them, made a desolate impression. The first fifteen was playing an away match, the grandest of its modest season, and Thursgood had gone with it in support, wearing a new hat & taking with him a busload of scrubbed boys. Only a smattering therefore was left in occupation; and the sashwindows of the main façades were unlit

Noone paid much attention when Jim arrived at Thursgood's: a sandy man with a criss crossed face. And if old Dover hadn't dropped dead at Taunton races, he would never have come at all. He came in mid-term, without an interview, sent in a hurry by one of the shiftier agencies specialising in supply-teachers for prep schools, to hold down old Dover's teaching, till someone suitable could be found. 'An Oxford man,' Thursgood told the common room without expression, on the eve of his arrival, 'a temporary measure. I understand we're his first appointment. He's not young, he comes from one of the professions.' And added, talking rather to the silence than to his audience: 'He's only till the end of term.' The announcement made, he turned gratefully

1.

No one paid much attention when Jim arrived at Thursgood's: a sandy man with a criss-crossed face. And if old Dover hadn't dropped dead at Taunton races, he would never have come at all. He came in mid-term, without an interview, sent in a hurry by one of the shiftier agencies specialising in supply teachers for prep schools, to hold down old Dover's teaching till someone suitable could be found. 'An Oxford man,' Thursgood told the common room without expression, on the eve of his arrival, 'a temporary measure. I understand we're his first appointment. He's not young, he comes from one of the professions.' And added, talking rather to the silence than to his audience: 'He's only till the end of term.' The announcement made, he turned gratefully to other things, leaving with his audience nevertheless an expectation as depressing as it was familiar: Jim was a poor white of the teaching world. He belonged to the same sad procession as the late Mrs. de Philo Loveday who had a Persian lamb coat and stood-in for junior divinity until her cheques began bouncing; or poor Mr. Acupar the white haired pianist, also a temporary, who had been called from choir practice unexpectedly to help the police with their enquiries; and for all anyone knew was helping them still, for he had not been heard of to this day, though his things were in a trunk in the cellar awaiting his instructions. Several of the staff were in favour of opening that trunk,

the ~~grey~~ hostility of that December dark suited him so well he might have ordered it. For he knew that bad weather makes strangers of us ~~all~~ all; ~~and~~ even the naturally curious forget to stare.

This new manuscript version is combined with a few pages of a (possibly older) typescript version, in which 'I' has already been replaced by 'Jim' in the typed layer: 'Jim was watching Tarr too' (page numbered '4a' by le Carré).

On 9 January le Carré made another handwritten version, deleting 'fat':

> It was early December when Tarr called, a Saturday about three. All day a ~~fat~~ yellow mist had been rolling down the bracken coombs of the Quantocks

This version was then typed out, and le Carré developed several aspects of the opening scene, emphasizing that 'Jim let Tarr wait, that was deliberate' (11 January 1972). But then, on 1 February 1972 (SEE FIG. 57), he decided to start differently, with Jim as the perceiving agent again, still playing referee at a rugby match at Thursgood's boys' school (in a newly handwritten version):

> Noone paid much attention when ~~he~~ Jim arrived at Thursgood's: a sandy man with a criss crossed face. ~~In fact~~ and And if old Dover hadn't dropped dead at Taunton races, ~~odds are~~ he would never have come ~~to Thursgood's~~ at all.

This too was typed out and le Carré then revised it with blue ink, cutting the first sentence:

> ~~No one paid much attention when Jim arrived at Thursgood's: a sandy man with a criss-crossed~~ handsom ~~face. And~~ The truth is, if old Dover hadn't dropped dead at Taunton races, ~~he~~ Jim would never had come ~~at~~ to Thursgood's at all.

By cutting that first sentence, le Carré had found his opening line. More than four months after he started writing this opening scene, he made yet another version:

> The truth is, if old Dover hadn't dropped dead at Taunton races, Jim would never had come to Thursgood's at all.

Later, le Carré just added that Dover was a major, but basically the novel's beginning or 'incipit' was by now established. It had taken him almost half a year to find it.

PREVIOUS SPREAD

57 John le Carré's revised handwritten opening scene of *Tinker Tailor Soldier Spy*, starting with 'Noone paid much attention' (Oxford, Bodleian Library, MS. le Carré 24)

58 Corrected typescript of the revised opening scene of John le Carré's *Tinker Tailor Soldier Spy* (Oxford, Bodleian Library, MS. le Carré 24)

A novel's or a play's beginning may also need to change when a work is being adapted for another medium. When Alan Bennett rewrote his play *The Madness of George III* to turn it into the film *The Madness of King George*, he cut the opening scene and moved it to a slightly later moment. The play opens with a historical assault on George III in 1786: Margaret Nicholson's failed attack with a blunt dessert knife. The dramatic effect is that the narrative is set in motion when she 'strikes him'. Bennett considered opening the film version with this scene of the 'attempted assassination', but 'done in dumb show' (SEE FIG. 59).

59 Alan Bennett's typewritten notes for *The Madness of King George*, 'One Beginning: The Attempted Assassination of George III by Margaret Nicholson (1786)' (Oxford, Bodleian Library, MS. Bennett 145, fol. 217r)

217

One Beginning: The Attempted Assassination of George III by Margaret Nicholson (1786).

The assassination done in dumb show. King on his throne. Queen. His many children. The Prince of Wales and the Duke of York (both in their twenties)..all in livery or court dress The politicians ..more soberly dressed.

Music over.

The king descends from the throne (which will serve later as the Speakers Chair and the chair of correction).

In the centre of a line of courtiers he advances towards the front of the stage where a woman pulls back a shawl to reveal a small knife.

She strikes at him. Tries to strike him again. There is confusion. She is seized. The king is not wounded. Examines the pathetic little knife. Laughs. Orders her released. Summons doctors. They examine her, indicate she is mad.

She is taken off to Bedlam.

Bells ringing. Sounds of rejoicing. King a back on the throne.

Or, once the attempt has been made does the Queen rush on to closely followed by the Princes ?

But he also indicated that this was only 'One Beginning'. In the end, he cut it. The director and he decided not to open with this dramatic scene, but to postpone it until after the long opening credits, more than five minutes into the movie. Instead, the film opens with a sequence of scenes of life at the court of George III running up to the opening of Parliament in 1788. This is certainly not a unique case of cutting and rewriting as a collaborative effort, as we will discuss in Chapter 8.

The sense of an ending

The incipit (Lat. 'it begins') is always a 'decisive and (in every sense) primordial' moment, according to Raymonde Debray Genette.[98] It is decisive because it sets up the initial narrative parameters (such as perspective, tone and focus) which 'determine the conditions for closure', as Niels Buch Leander notes in *The Sense of a Beginning*.[99] Leander's title alludes to Frank Kermode's critical study *The Sense of an Ending*. Kermode compares the notion of narrative closure to a clock's 'tick-tock', which he sees as a model of plot-making, 'an organization which humanises time by giving it a form'.[100] Time is just successive, not organized. As human beings, we feel a rather universal urge to organize it, and this applies to readers in particular: when we hear a tick, we are eager to hear the tock that is supposed to follow and that gives us a sense of closure. 'Tick is a humble genesis, tock a feeble apocalypse', as Kermode puts it, and the interval 'must be purged of simple chronicity'.[101] As a consequence, a story's ending or explicit (from Latin, *explicitum est* 'it is unrolled') can be arguably even more decisive than the incipit. And for a writer it can be just as difficult to find the right ending as it is to find the first sentence. Debray Genette studied the way Flaubert wrote the ending of his story 'A Simple Heart' ('Un Cœur simple') and concludes that the double function of the story's end is 'to close the plot and to open reflection'.[102] To accomplish this, Flaubert mainly had to cut. He needed several versions to gradually eliminate all judgemental phrases so that it is up to the reader to decide what to think of the final image: the protagonist's vision of the Holy Spirit in the shape of her stuffed parrot. Flaubert leaves it up to the reader to determine whether this is ironic or not. Finding this very fine balance was what it took to find the right ending, *la fin juste* as it were.

Similarly, to close the plot and to open reflection, Raymond Chandler needed several versions to finish his detective novel *The Long Good-bye* (1953). The sixth novel featuring the private investigator Philip Marlowe focuses on the alcoholic war veteran Terry Lennox. Marlowe gives him a ride across the border to Tijuana, only to discover afterwards that Lennox is the prime suspect in the murder of his wealthy wife. After three days of interrogation by the police on suspicion of having helped a suspected murderer, Marlowe is released. Lennox has been reported to have committed suicide in Mexico, and when Marlowe arrives home he finds a letter from Lennox containing a 'portrait of Madison' (a $5,000 note). After a complex plot, Marlowe is visited by a Mexican man who calls himself Señor Maioranos and claims to have been present when Lennox died in his hotel room. He turns out to be Lennox, who has had cosmetic surgery. While Lennox tries to make amends for the trouble he has caused, Marlowe simply opens the safe and returns the 'portrait of Madison'.

The archive contains several 'discarded' pages. The book delivers what the title promises. The ending really was a long good-bye. Chandler typed it out and then reread it, discarding numerous lines (SEE FIG. 60). He used a pencil to underscore only the lines that he thought worth keeping. For instance, when Marlowe tells Lennox he won't say good-bye – 'I said it to you when it meant something' – the earlier version spends several lines on a description of Lennox's reaction: 'He frowned and suddenly rubbed the tips of his fingers along the side of his face – the way he used to do when it had no feeling, the way I had been doing myself for a while. <u>There was a glint of tears in his eyes</u>' (100r; numbered '831' by Chandler). In the published version Chandler just kept the underlined sentence: 'There was suddenly a glint of tears in his eyes. He put his dark glasses back on quickly.'[103]

The final paragraph, on the other hand, was originally shorter (SEE FIG. 61). After Lennox has said good-bye, he 'turned away quickly and went out. I watched the door close and listened to his steps going away. After a little while I couldn't hear them, but I kept on listening. / Don't ask me why. I couldn't tell you' (101r; numbered '833' by Chandler). In two revision campaigns, one with a red ballpoint pen, one with a blue one, Chandler kept making changes: 'I kept listening anyway. As if he might come back … But he didn't.' And in the final version the good-bye became even longer:

OVERLEAF

60 Discarded typescript pages of Raymond Chandler's novel *The Long Good-bye* (Oxford, Bodleian Library, Dep. Chandler 5, fol. 100r)

61 Raymond Chandler's discarded typescript pages of the ending of *The Long Good-bye* (Oxford, Bodleian Library, Dep. Chandler 5, fol. 101r)

"There's more of us than youthink. But the way you said it is funny. Real funny. You bought a lot of me, Terry. For a smile and a nod and a wave of the hand and a few quiet drinks in a bar. For a little charm. For a change of pace in between your more expensive moments. So long, amigo. I won't say goodbye. I said it to you when it meant something."

"I guess I came back too late," he said."But these plastic jobs take time."

"Would you have come at all if I hadn't smoked you out?"

He frowned and suddenly rubbed the tips of his fin gers along the side of his face--the way he used to do when it had no feeling, the way I had been doing myself for a while. There was a glint of tears in his eyes.

"Don't you enjoy it just a little?"

He stood up. I stood up too. He put out his lean hand. I shook it.

"Goodbye, Senor Maioranos. Nice to have known you for a little while."

"Goodbye."

He turned away quickly and went out. I watched the door close and listened to his steps going away. After a little while I couldn't hear them, but I kept on listening.

Don't ask me why. I couldn't tell you.

RC

July 11,1953.

> I kept on listening anyway. What for? Did I want him to stop suddenly and turn and come back and talk me out of the way I felt? Well, he didn't. That was the last I saw of him. / I never saw any of them again – except the cops. No way has yet been invented to say good-bye to them.[104]

Or an alternative ending

Jane Austen's novel *Persuasion* similarly has an alternative ending. Whether or not she revised it because she thought it 'tame and flat', as her nephew J.E. Austen-Leigh suggested, the fact that she cut it is the reason why we still have the manuscript of the original ending (the last two chapters).[105] All the manuscripts of Austen's published novels appear to have been destroyed once they were typeset (see Chapter 1). But because she rewrote the ending of *Persuasion*, the original was not discarded. It is held at the British Library. Most critics agree that the published ending is better than the original one, but that makes it all the more interesting to have a look at the cut version (freely accessible online at Jane Austen's Fiction Manuscripts, janeausten.ac.uk) as it gives us a rare insight into the way Austen worked. The manuscript fragment, written in the summer of 1816, is a single gathering of sixteen leaves.

The heroine is the twenty-seven-year-old Anne Elliot. Due to debts, her father is obliged to lease their home, Kellynch Hall, to Admiral Croft, whose wife happens to be the sister of Captain Frederick Wentworth. Anne and Wentworth had been engaged seven or eight years earlier until the engagement was broken after her family and friends persuaded her to end the relationship. So, many years later, they meet again, both single. Wentworth overhears a conversation in which Anne tells his friend Captain Harville that, according to her, women tend to hang on to lost love for much longer than men do. As he realizes there might still be a possibility for them to be a couple, he writes a very moving letter that plays an instrumental role in their eventual engagement. That crucial letter is part of the penultimate chapter. In the cancelled chapters, however, the story ends without this letter. Instead, Austen made the jovial Admiral Croft suddenly coax Anne into calling on his wife, suggesting that she has 'something particular to say'. His unexpected form of waylaying is rather out of character. Inside, it is not Mrs Croft but Captain Wentworth who is awaiting her, telling her that the Crofts heard she was betrothed to a distant relation of hers and that they are therefore willing to give up Kellynch Hall so that Anne and her fiancé can move in. When Anne tells Wentworth that the rumours of this engagement are false, they reveal their true love for each other.

This ending is not bad, but it involves the admiral stepping out of character to create a situation in which the couple can be alone in his office. This is almost too convenient to be an Austen novel. In Austen's works, a couple's happiness seldom involves only the two of them. And so, in the revised version, Austen expands the time frame for the reconciliation and brings in almost all the main characters again at the end, which involves more obstacles. But, thanks to the obstacles, the moment Wentworth can declare his love by means of his letter becomes more powerful. And at the same time, Austen uses the moment to demonstrate the power of the written word:

> You pierce my soul. I am half agony, half hope. Tell me not that I am too late, that such precious feelings are gone for ever. I offer myself to you again with a heart even more your own than when you almost broke it, eight years and a half ago. Dare not say that man forgets sooner than woman, that his love has an earlier death. I have loved none but you.[106]

To be able to make that ending so powerful, Austen did have to write the blander version and realize why it was too bland. In that sense, the ending of *Persuasion* is persuasive, so to speak, thanks to the cancelled chapters.

by a gracious answer, & a more liberal full view of her face than she had yet bestowed.

Unused to exert himself, & happy in contem-
-plating her, he then sat in silence for some minutes longer, while Tom Musgrave was chatter-
-ing to Elizth., till they were interrupted by Nanny's half opening the door & putting

8

EDITORS' & OTHERS' CUTS

Chapter 7th

It was on a dreary night of November that I beheld ~~the frame on whic~~ ~~my~~ man compleated, ~~and~~ with an anxiety that almost amounted to agony I collected instruments of life around me ~~and endeavoured~~ that I might infuse a spark of being into the lifeless thing that lay at my feet. It was already one in the morning, the rain pattered dismally against the window panes & my candle was nearly burnt out, when by the glimmer of the half extinguished light I saw the dull yellow eye of the creature open ~~—~~ It breathed hard, and a convulsive motion agitated its limbs.

~~But how~~ How can I describe my emotion at this catastrophe, or how delineate the wretch whom with such infinite pains and care I had endavoured to form. His limbs were in proportion and I had selected his features ~~&~~ as ~~handsome~~ ~~handsome~~ ~~Handsome~~ Beautiful beautiful. Great God! His yellow ~~dun~~ skin scarcely covered the work of muscles and arteries beneath; his hair was of a lustrous black & flowing and his teeth of a pearly whiteness but ~~these~~ luxuriances only ~~formed~~ formed a more horrid contrast with his watry eyes that seemed almost of the same colour as the dun white sockets in which they were set,

Authors are not the only ones who cut. The theatre and the film industry typically involve forms of collaborative creativity, which is less private than the writing of, say, a poem or a novel. Still, if you happen to live with a famous author and want to write a novel yourself, it would not be a bad idea to ask for their advice once in a while. Mary Shelley (1797–1851) started working on her novel *Frankenstein* when she was only eighteen years old, and the manuscripts show several traces of the suggestions made by Percy Bysshe Shelley (1792–1822). Take the famous chapter that starts with 'It was on a dreary night of November that I beheld my man completed with an anxiety that almost amounted to agony' (see fig. 62). The manuscript shows how Mary was in two minds about the spelling of the word 'completed' ('compleated' or 'completed'). She makes Victor Frankenstein describe how his creature came to life.

At first, it is still 'the lifeless thing that lay at my feet'. But then, at 'one in the morning', he sees 'the dull yellow eye of the creature open':

> How can I describe my emotion at this catastrophe; or how delineate the wretch whom with such infinite pains and care I had endeavoured to form. His limbs were in proportion and I had selected his features as handsome. Handsome, Great God!

The word 'handsome' suggests the notion of 'good-looking' and emphasizes the concrete, physical shape of the creature. Percy appears to have tried to emphasize the more abstract allegory of creation, by suggesting to Mary she change 'handsome' into 'beautiful', twice. And she did. The published version reads: 'I had selected his features as beautiful. Beautiful! Great God!' Beauty was a key concept in Romantic poetry. 'Beauty is truth, truth beauty', John Keats wrote one year after the publication of *Frankenstein*. But, of course, whether Frankenstein had selected his creature's features as 'handsome' or

62 Mary Shelley's manuscript of *Frankenstein*, with annotations by Percy Bysshe Shelley (Oxford, Bodleian Library, MS. Abinger c. 56, Draft Notebook A, fol. 21r)

'beautiful', the result was equally ugly – especially 'his watry eyes that seemed almost of the same colour as the dun white sockets in which they were set' (SEE FIG. 62).

Sometimes authors count on confidants or others to kill their darlings. An illustrative case is the collaboration between Alan Bennett and theatre director Nicholas Hytner, first on the play *The Madness of George III* and then the movie *The Madness of King George*. In 1992 Bennett wrote an account of their collaboration, published in the *London Review of Books*. After having worked on the play for about a year, he decided in April 1991 that he needed some feedback: 'knowing it was far from finished and in some despair, I put it through Nicholas Hytner's door'.[107] Again, it was especially the ending that caused most trouble. Hytner wrote in his memoirs about Bennett's writing that 'Alan's endings often take time to emerge'.[108] Bennett studied history at Oxford and the historical accuracy of the play was, initially, of paramount importance to him. Hytner, as a director, was more concerned about the dramatic tension and saw to it that the play 'worked' on stage. What Hytner, like most people, did not know initially was that the historical King George III did not just 'go mad', but that there had been a period of two decades in which he had recovered. That historical fact was important to Bennett. In the original version of the play, the King's recovery after the first bout of madness constituted the end. The doctors are quarrelling over the King's recovery and who deserves most credit for it. At that point, Bennett introduces an anachronistic character: Doctor Hunter, 'a modern doctor comes down the steps in white coat and stethoscope' (SEE FIG. 63).[109]

This twentieth-century doctor explains to his eighteenth-century colleagues that the King was not mad, but that he had been suffering from porphyria. Bennett had read about this explanation in a book by Richard Hunter and Ida Macalpine, titled *George III and the Mad-Business* (1969). One of the authors of this book thus got the chance to time-travel, as it were, and tell his truth to the Georgian ignoramuses. This was followed by a discussion that was 'long and detailed, too much so for this stage of the play', according to Bennett himself.[110] In the end, he made the King come out and describe how he would eventually end up mad anyway. While 'The DOCTORS are still arguing', the King jovially addresses them – 'Still at it, what, what'[111] – and describes his future as follows:

> But call it porphyria or what you will, I ended up mad anyway. Had another do in 1802. Got over it, then again in 1810, only that was it. Finished up blind, deaf. What, what. Died in 1820.[112]

63 Early typescript of Alan Bennett's *The Madness of George III*, introducing an anachronistic, twentieth-century character, called Dr Hunter (Oxford, Bodleian Library, MS. Bennett 146, fol. 334r)

334

2/51

BAKER Another satisfied patient!

WARREN Quite, though I find it dispiriting on such occasions that it is the Deity who gets the credit rather than his chosen instruments, the medical profession.

PEPYS He might have recovered without us.

WARREN In which case I hope you'll be returning your fee.

BAKER Willis isn't getting a fee, are you Willis.
An annuity of £1000 a year.
Very nice.

WILLIS No doubt had ~~the patient not~~ His Majesty not recovered you would have received more.

WARREN That's a scandalous suggestion.
If you were a fellow of the royal College...

BAKER Whivh you never will be..

WARREN I would have you expelled.
It was a physical illness with physical causes ~~and~~ cured by physical means. A distemper which passed.
All your cultivation of the will and talking to the patient made not a haporth of difference. It was a disease of the body.

WILLIS It was a disease of the understanding.

HUNTER, a modern doctor, comes down the steps in white coat and stethoscope.

HUNTER Actually it was neither. Or it was both.
Did none of you look at the urine.

PEPYS I looked at the stool which was often quite hard to see ~~because the urine was quite~~ dark.
until one had poured away the urine. So dark.

HUNTER And did that tell you nothing ?

QUEEN : Yes, sir.

KING : There is something about you...

QUEEN : (letting down her hair) I am grey now, sir. Grey as an old mouse.

KING : Oh well. It is no matter.

QUEEN : I have lost what little share of beauty I once possessed.

KING : Still, you're a good little pudding.

QUEEN : When you were ill, it was said by some that had you led a...a normal life...it might not have happened.

KING : A normal life?

QUEEN : Other women, sir.

KING : Kicked over the traces, you mean, hey! No life is without its regrets. Yet none is without consolations. You are a good little woman, Mrs King. And we have been happy, have we not?

QUEEN : Yes, Mr King, we have.

KING : And shall be again. And shall be again.

Church bells, etc.
~~The KING and QUEEN emerge in IDA MCALPINE draws curtain cutting off the bedroom. She is followed by FORTNUM and PAPANDIEK off duty. BRAUN and FITZROY look on.~~

DR MACALPINE : ~~IDA~~ : He's better, of course, but he's not cured. And he's not going to be cured. Urine, young man. You were quite right.

FORTNUM : Blue?

BRAUN : Purple.

IDA : Exactly. The colour of porphyry. Hence the name of the disease. I wrote a book about it.

Change to: DR. MACALPINE throughout

She holds the book up. Before PAPANDIEK gets a chance to look at it, FITZROY ~~takes it.~~ comes up behind her and takes it.

The last page of the typescript was a rather moralistic ending, spoken by the King:

> The real lesson, if I may say so, gentlemen, is that what makes an illness perilous is celebrity. Or in my case royalty. In the ordinary course of things doctors want their patients to recover. Their reputation, their fees, their credit depends on it. But if the patient is rich or royal, powerful or famous other considerations enter in. There are many parties interested apart from the interested party, the patient. … I tell you, if you're poorly it's safer to be poor and ordinary. Though not too poor, of course. What, what?[113]

In his account, Bennett wrote that he was fond of this ending, immediately admitting that it was 'determinedly untheatrical' and basically a rather elaborate version of saying 'too many cooks spoil the broth', but this was the nearest he said he could get to extracting a message from the play. From a theatrical point of view, however, Hytner recalls that, during rehearsals, Nigel Hawthorne (the actor who played the King) came to him to protest about this scene, because he felt he could not play it 'after taking the audience through a highly emotional and naturalistic evening'.[114] And the author fully understood: 'Nigel Hawthorne felt, I think rightly, that he couldn't step out of his character so easily and that if he did the audience would feel cheated.'[115]

Bennett therefore rewrote the ending. But he still could not kill his darling, the anachronistic introduction of a twentieth-century doctor. Instead of simply omitting the modern doctor in white coat and stethoscope, he replaced Doctor Hunter with Doctor Macalpine, named after the co-author of the same source of inspiration, *George III and the Mad-Business* (SEE FIG. 64).

> ~~IDA~~ DR MACALPINE: He's better, of course, but he's not cured. And he's not going to be cured. Urine, young man. You were quite right.
> FORTNUM: Blue?
> BRAUN: Purple.
> ~~IDA~~ DR MACALPINE: Exactly. The colour of porphyry. Hence the name of the disease. I wrote a book about it.[116]

Agreeing with Hawthorne, the director still felt that the device of the anachronistic doctors did not work: 'the rest of the play so convincingly and truthfully appeared to deliver the English court 1788–89, that the appearance of a woman in a white coat was not going to be bought.'[117]

64 Revised typescript of Alan Bennett's *The Madness of George III*, introducing another anachronistic, twentieth-century character, called Dr Macalpine, who claims the King had been suffering from porphyria (Oxford, Bodleian Library, MS. Bennett 146, fol. 588r)

In the 'Cut version',[118] therefore, the King gets the last word at the steps of St Paul's, but no longer to teach the 'real lesson':

> You may tell Dr Willis that the ceremony will not be such a burden as the want of ceremony has been. And do not look at me, sir. Presume not I am the thing I was. I am not the patient. Be off, sir. Back to your sheep and your pigs. The King is himself again.[119]

For the movie, Bennett suggested a 'possible cut' (147:641/642) at several instances. As to the ending, he did add two alternatives to the first draft of the film script.[120] The first keeps holding on to the introduction of Ida Macalpine, who tells the doctors what according to her was the cause of the King's condition (porphyria). Instead of introducing her as a modern doctor in a white coat with stethoscope, she is described rather awkwardly as 'a small dumpy woman, in odd clothes, very Jewish and with a Viennese accent. She is sitting with a modern brief case open on her knee making notes' (147:356/357). She tells Captain Greville that the bluish purple colour of the King's urine is 'The colour of porphyry. Hence the name of the disease. I wrote a book about it' (147:356). When Greville asks Macalpine 'You're sure about this', Bennett makes her reply, not without a touch of irony: 'Of course I'm sure. I'm a doctor' (SEE FIG. 65).[121]

The second alternative ending suggests including the information about porphyria in the credits and also makes a concession to another objection of Hytner's. The director had wanted to make the Prince of Wales more eager to take over from his father. In the original draft, the Prince of Wales was just a puppet in the political power play between the Whigs and the Tories (represented respectively by Charles James Fox and William Pitt the Younger). When Hytner and Bennett discussed the movie adaptation, the director suggested 'making the P of W cleverer'.[122] According to Hytner, they needed to create 'a much stronger impression than in the play that the P of W is gaining control of Windsor and of the King' (524). They kept coming back to the same issue: 'Usual thing: P of W needs beefing up' (526). Hytner recognized what the cause of the problem was: he had to convince the author to distort history to increase narrative tension.[123] Bennett, from his side, later presented this discussion as a battle with fatalities and collateral damage: 'One casualty of the rewrites was strict historical truth.'[124] But afterwards he did admit that 'the play only works if the antipathy between father and son, never far below the surface with all the Hanoverian Kings, is sharpened and the Prince made less sympathetic.'[125]

65 Alan Bennett's alternative ending for the screenplay of *The Madness of King George* (Oxford, Bodleian Library, MS. Bennett 147, fol. 360r)

9 359

He has another attack in 1802 and finally takes leave of his senses in 1802 1810, dying deaf and blind in 1820.

166 360

DOCTOR MACALPINE has gathered up her belongings and is going out. GREVILLE dazzled by the light from the windows can't quite see her clearly, or whether she's there at all.

GREVILLE Madam.

MACALPINE stops.

You're sure about this.

MACALPINE Of course I'm sure. I am a doctor.

OR

Alternatively this information can be included in the credits:

'George III may not have been clinically mad but suffering from a metabolic disorder which turns the urine blue and produces symptoms similar to dementia. He had another attack in 1802 and in 1810 finally took leave of his senses.'

PRINCE OF WALES. We have turned the key on the King. He'll come back no more, I promise you.

Nor did he and though deaf and blind he lived on until 1820 he never resumed the throne.

~~[illegible]~~

~~[illegible] on the steps of St Paul's~~

Shot of a barred window at WINDSOR and a face behind it.

The case of *The Madness of King George* shows that some authors really count on editors and directors to kill their darlings. And if they don't, there is always the distributor to give further advice – in this case the Samuel Goldwyn Company, making suggestions by fax. Hytner later told Duncan Wu in an interview that, in the theatre, his role as a director was indeed that of a facilitator, or even a translator – 'the translator of what's on the page onto the stage'.[126]

Lost in translation

That role of a translator – literally this time – is what T.S. Eliot (1888–1965) played to the French author Saint-John Perse (1887–1975). Perse, a pseudonym of Alexis Leger, born in Guadeloupe, wrote a long poem titled *Anabase*, which was published in 1924, two years after the publication of Eliot's *The Waste Land*. Impressed by the poem, Eliot took on the task of translating it and asked Saint-John Perse on 15 January 1927 if he would be so kind as to have a look at his translation, accompanied by a list of questions for the author. It would take Perse two years to respond, but in the meantime he found Valery Larbaud willing to take a look at it and to reply to Eliot's queries. Larbaud's eleven handwritten pages of 'Answers and explanations', kept at the Fondation Saint-John Perse (FSJP) in Aix-en-Provence, contain some helpful suggestions. For instance, section IV of the poem opens with the foundation of 'la ville' (the City), which according to the French text was 'placée au matin sous les labiales d'un nom *pur*'.[127] Eliot translates this as 'placed in the morning under the labials of a *sanctified* name. Larbaud suggests: 'instead of "sanctified", would holy do? (the meaning is: religiously spotless)'.[128] And Eliot indeed changed it to 'the labials of a *holy* name' in the published version.[129] When Saint-John Perse describes the colour of the river as 'une couleur de sauterelles écrasées dans leur *sève*',[130] Eliot originally translated this as a 'colour of grasshoppers crushed in their *pus*'.[131] Larbaud commented diplomatically, wary of speculating about authorial intention and speaking instead of the text's intention: '"Pus" does not seem to correspond to the intention of the text: if "sap" is impossible, would not "juice" do? (as of herbs or fruits).'[132] Eliot revised his translation accordingly and it appeared as the 'colour of grasshoppers crushed in their *sap*'.[133]

Still, Larbaud's suggestions were not entirely sufficient for Eliot, as he wrote in a letter to Marguerite Caetani, Princess of Bassiano (17 March

1927); as soon as he received Perse's comments, he promised he would use both Larbaud's and Perse's annotations for his revision and send a final version. Perse was apparently not in a hurry, but he did take Eliot's queries seriously and his replies were deemed of such hermeneutic value that they were incorporated in the Pléiade edition of the complete works of Saint-John Perse. Marguerite Caetani helped Perse by writing out his comments on Eliot's typescript, starting with a long annotation next to the title (SEE FIG. 66).

Perse wanted Eliot to cut the Greek Σ which he used in his translation of the title. The comment starts with 'better in Latin letters' and continues in French, noting that it has nothing to do with Xenophon ('Rien à voir avec Xénophon') and that the word is used simply in the etymological sense of an inward expedition ('dans le simple sens étmologique de: "expédition vers l'intérieur"') – which adds an ironic dimension to an odd statement in Eliot's preface. As the manuscript shows, he clearly needed to be told that the title did not refer to Xenophon, and yet he writes in his preface: 'I did not need to be told, after one reading, that the word *anabasis* has no particular reference to Xenophon or the journey of the Ten Thousand, no particular reference to *Asia Minor*; and that no map of its migrations could be drawn up.'[134] He continues by introducing the word 'wastes' and thus presenting the poem as an echo of his own *The Waste Land*: 'Mr Perse is using the word *anabasis* in the same literal sense in which Xenophon himself used it. The poem is a series of images of migration, of conquest of vast spaces in Asiatic *wastes*, of destruction and foundation of cities and civilisations.'[135]

With Caetani's help, Perse continued to comment on Eliot's translation – Perse with only very sparse marks in grey pencil, Caetani with more elaborate suggestions in red ink. Because of the abundance of red comments on the poem's first section (fol. 03r), for instance, it is easy to overlook the only words in pencil: 'comme un sel' (like salt) (SEE FIG. 67), which read like the author's modest protest: please don't cut this phrase. In the typescript, Eliot had indeed translated 'l'idée pure *comme un sel* tient ses assises dans le jour'[136] as 'the pure idea holds its assize in the day' (fol. 03r). Caetani 'translated' the pencil mark into a concrete suggestion in red ink and also changed 'day' into 'light'. Eliot then changed the line into 'the idea pure *as salt* holds its assize in the light time'[137] – revising with the author's help and reinstating one of the darlings that had unduly been killed.

OVERLEAF

66 T.S. Eliot's translation of Saint-John Perse's poem 'Anabasis', with a long annotation next to the title, noting that the title had nothing to do with Xenophon (Oxford, Bodleian Library, MS. Don. C. 23/2, fol. 1r)

67 T.S. Eliot's translation of Saint-John Perse's poem 'Anabasis', with the words 'comme un sel' in pencil among the many corrections in red ink (Oxford, Bodleian Library, MS. Don. C. 23/2, fol. 3r)

1

8

A N A B A Σ I Σ

S S

better in Latin letters

Le mot "anabase", neutralisé
dans ma pensée jusqu'à
l'effacement d'un terme usuel,
ne doit plus suggérer aucune
association d'idées classiques.
Rien à voir avec Xénophon.
Le mot est employé ici abstraitement
et incorporé au français courant
avec toute la discrétion nécessaire
— monnaie usagée et signe fiduciaire —
dans le ~~sens~~ simple sens étymologique de:
"expédition vers l'intérieur",
avec une signification à la fois
géographique et spirituelle
(ambiguïté voulue)

poem of

ST. J. PERSE .

Translated into English by

T.S. ELIOT

From T.S. Eliot, 17 Jan., 1931.

I.

I have built myself, with strength and dignity have I built myself on three seasons, and it promises well, the soil whereon I have established my Law.

Our burnished arms are fair in the morning and behind us the sea is fair. This fruitless earth given over to our horses

is more to us that this incorruptible sky. The Sun is unmentioned but his power is amongst us

and the sea at morning like a pride of the spirit.

Power, who sang on our ways of bivouac and vigil!. At the pure idea of dawn what know we of the primogeniture of dream?

Yet one more year among you! Master of the Grain, Master of the Salt, and the commonwealth on an even beam!

I shall not hail the people of another shore. I shall not trace the divers quarters of cities. I would simply live among you.

Glory to the threshold of the tents, and my strength among you, and the pure idea holds its assize in the day.

...So I haunted the City of your dreams, and I established on the desolate markets the pure communication of my soul, among you

invisible and insistent as a fire of thorns in the wind.

Power, you sang on our roads of honour. The spears of the spirit press toward the pleasure of salt... With salt shall I revive the dead mouths of desire!

by a gracious answer, & a more full view
of her face than she had yet bestowed.
Unused to exert himself, & happy in contem-
-plating her, he then sat in silence for some
minutes longer, while Tom Musgrave was chatter-
-ing to Elizth, till they were interrupted by Nanny's

9
REPURPOSING

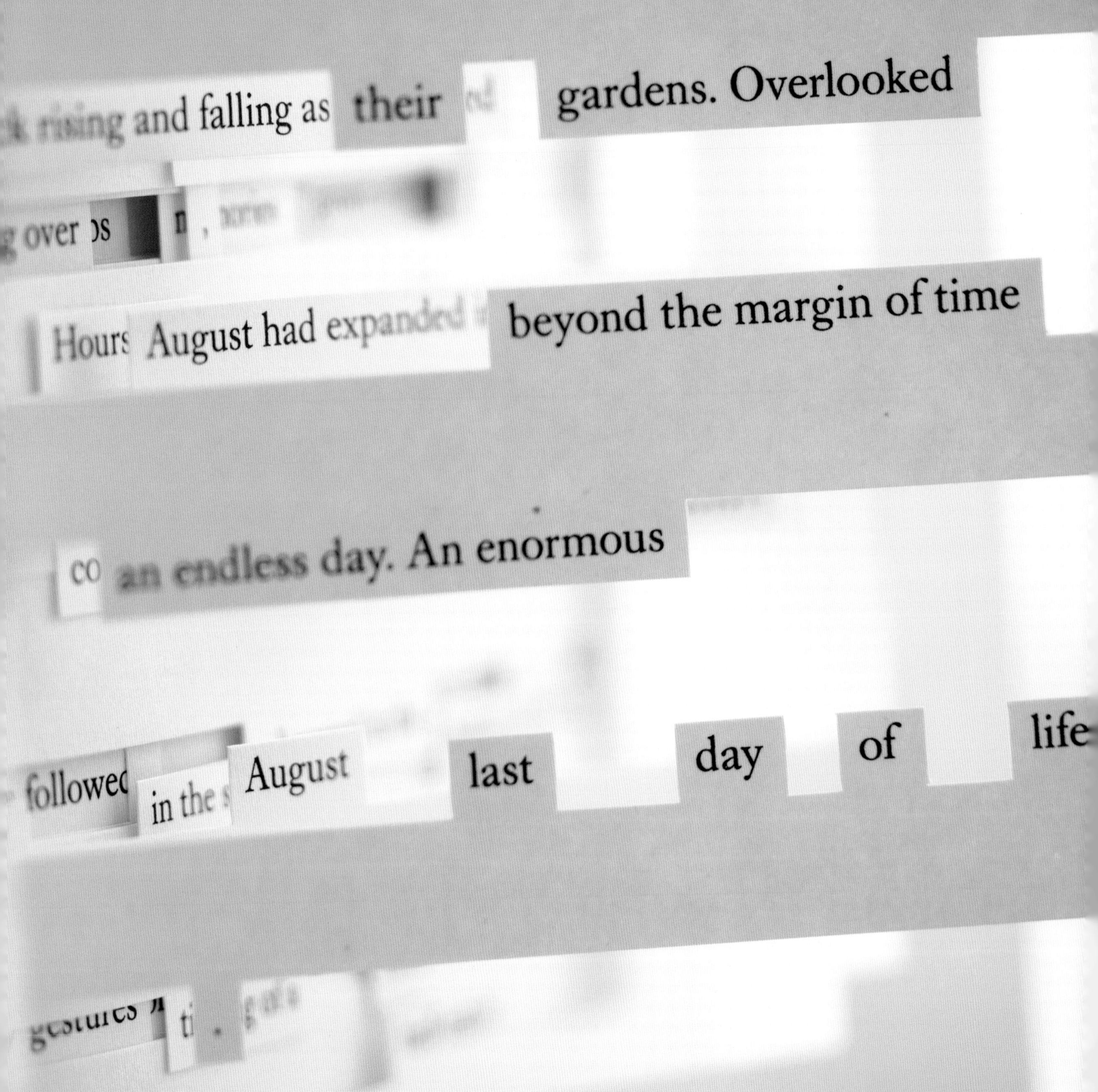

rising and falling as
their
gardens. Overlooked
over
Hours
August had
beyond the margin of time
an endless day. An enormous
followed
in the
August
last
day
of
life

Cutting and pasting often happens within a single work, moving a verse, a stanza, a sentence, a paragraph or even a chapter to another place. It also occurs within an author's œuvre, as when for instance Alexander Pope cut the phrase 'damned to fame' from *An Essay on Criticism* and repurposed it in *The Dunciad*. But sometimes part of the genesis of a work can be found in the work of another author. This kind of 'allogenesis' applies to the case of Jonathan Safran Foer's *Tree of Codes*, which is made from Bruno Schulz's novel *The Street of Crocodiles*.[138] Schulz (1892–1942) was a Polish writer, killed by the Gestapo during the Second World War. All of his manuscripts were destroyed. As a form of homage, Foer created a die-cut book, omitting major parts of the story. The phrases are literally cut from the text and printed as such, with holes in the text on every page (see fig. 68).

One of the things Foer consistently cut was the name of the housemaid Adela. Her name does not appear in the book anymore. The result is that the female pronouns, even the ones that originally referred to Adela, now all refer to the narrator's mother, who has consequently become a changed character. The same principle was applied to the title: *The Street of Crocodiles* became *Tree of Codes*.

Cut & paste

In a different way, Mary Shelley cut a passage from one of Percy's notebooks. His Geneva Notebook is filled with drawings of mountains and lakes, notes and drafts for his poem *Mont Blanc* (see figs 69 & 70).

68 Jonathan Safran Foer's *Tree of Codes*, made from Bruno Schulz's novel *The Street of Crocodiles* (1934)

On 23 June 1816 Percy noted in his notebook (SEE FIG. 71):

> ~~I~~ We could observe its path thro the chasm of the mountains & the glens of the lower hills, ~~until~~ The mountains here come closer to the lake, ~~& we could see the eastern boundary enclose its waters so that~~ & we approached the amphitheatre ~~which~~ of mountains which forms its eastern boundary. The spire of Evian shone ~~in~~ under the woods that surrounded & the range of mountain above mountain which overhung it.[139]

This passage was torn from the notebook. Charles E. Robinson points out that this fragment was almost literally incorporated in the draft of *Frankenstein*, in Mary Shelley's hand:

> The sun~~k~~ sunk lower in the heavens // we passed by the river Drance & observed its path through the chasm of the mountains & the glens of the lower hills. The ~~Mountains~~ Alps here come closer to the lake & we approached the amphitheatre of mountains that forms its eastern boundary. The spire of Evian shone under the woods that surrounded it & the range of mountain above mountain which overhung it.[140]

69 Sketch of Lake Geneva from Percy Bysshe Shelley's Geneva Notebook (Oxford, Bodleian Library, MS. Shelley adds. e. 16, pp. 44–5)

70 Percy Bysshe Shelley's Geneva Notebook (Oxford, Bodleian Library, MS. Shelley adds. e. 16, pp. 56–7)

71 Manuscript page torn from Percy Bysshe Shelley's Geneva Notebook and used for a descriptive paragraph in *Frankenstein* (Oxford, Bodleian Library, MS. Shelley Adds. c. 4)

72 Mary Shelley's manuscript of *Frankenstein*, containing a description of the lake and mountains surrounding Evian, based on Percy Shelley's Geneva Notebook (Oxford, Bodleian Library, MS. Abinger c. 57, p. 162, fol. 73v)

73 Mary Shelley's fair copy of *Frankenstein* containing a descriptive paragraph based on Percy Shelley's Geneva Notebook (Oxford, Bodleian Library, MS. Abinger c. 58, fol. 6r)

As Percy read the manuscript and made suggestions, he also (re)read this passage and made a small suggestion: to change 'the range of mountain above mountain which it overhung' into 'the range of mountain above mountain *by* which it *was* overhung' (SEE FIG. 72).[141] And that is how it appeared in the fair copy (SEE FIG. 73) and in the published novel (the penultimate paragraph of volume 3, chapter 5 in the 1818 edition; chapter 22 in the 1831 edition).

162) we passed by the river Drance & observed its
path ~~through~~ the chasm of the mountains
& the glens of the lower hills. The ~~mountains~~
Alps here come closer to the lake & we approach
ed ~~the~~ amphitheatre of mountains that
forms its ~~eastern~~ boundary. The spire
of Evian shone under the woods that
surrounded it & the range of mountain
above mountain by which it was overhung ~~it~~.
The wind which had hitherto carried
us along with amazing rapidity sunk
at sunset to a gentle breeze – the light
air just ruffled the water & caused a
pleasant motion among the trees as we
approached the shore it wafted the
most delightful scent of flowers & hay.
The ~~saw~~ sun sunk beneath the horizon
as we landed and as I touched the shore
I felt ~~those~~ cares and fears revive
which ~~& I had forgotten while on the~~
~~water~~. soon were to clasp me & cling to me
forever.

ges but it continually gave place to distraction and reverie.

The sun sunk lower in the heavens; we passed the river Drance and observed its path through the chasms of the higher and the glens of the lower hills. The ~~[illegible]~~ Alps here come closer to the lake and we approached the amphi- ~~the~~ theatre of mountains which forms the eastern boundary of the lake. The spire of Evian shone ~~unde~~ under the woods that surrounded it and the range of mountain above mountain by which it was overhung.

The wind which had hitherto carried us a- long with amazing rapidity sunk at sunset to a

74 Book of hours from Normandy, France (c.1440–1450) (Oxford, Bodleian Library, Bodleian MS. Auct. d. inf. 2. 11, fol. 7r)

75 Postcard poem by Philip Larkin, sent to Monica Jones. The postcard features illuminations from the book of hours (shown in fig. 74). (Oxford, Bodleian Library, MS. Eng. c. 7445, fol. 54)

Cut & pasted from the past

Sometimes the archive can play a role in new forms of literary cutting and repurposing. In the early 1980s the Bodleian's bookshop offered postcards based on colourful images in a medieval book of hours, kept in the Special Collections (SEE FIG. 74).[142] It dates from the mid-fifteenth century (between 1440 and 1450), is written in French and Latin, and was produced in France.

For every month of the year, it shows an illustration of a typical human activity during that month, next to an image relating to a sign of the zodiac. The Bodleian cropped these images from the book of hours, reproduced them as postcards and presented them in the bookshop. Philip Larkin was one of the customers who bought a postcard of each month. Every month, inspired by the image on the front, he would write a poem on the back, which he would send to his partner, Monica Jones.[143] The poems can therefore be read as a form of ekphrasis – descriptions of a work of art. In July 1982, he sent her a poem under the sign of Leo (SEE FIG. 75):

Long lion days
Start with white haze.
By midday you meet
A hammer of heat –
Whatever was sown
Now fully grown;
Whatever conceived
Now fully leaved,
Abounding, ablaze –
O long lion days![144]

When this poem is cut off from the material on which it is written, as in a collection of poetry of a collected-works edition,[145] it lends itself to various interpretations and associations. Thus, it has been linked to Britain's imperial past. In his book on *Poetry and the Nation State*, Tom Paulin – after mentioning icons of patriotic devotion in English culture, such as bows and arrows, cricket bats and oak trees – reads the midday 'hammer of heat' in Larkin's poem as 'a martial memory of imperial high noon'.[146] This association with the British Empire is less self-evident when the poem is read on the back of a postcard, showing a colourful fragment from a medieval book of hours made in France. The postcard is postmarked 22 July 1982. Moreover, on the postcard, Larkin signed the poem with 'Ted', which turns it into a parody of Ted Hughes's elemental nature poetry and invites alternative readings to 'a martial memory of imperial high noon'.

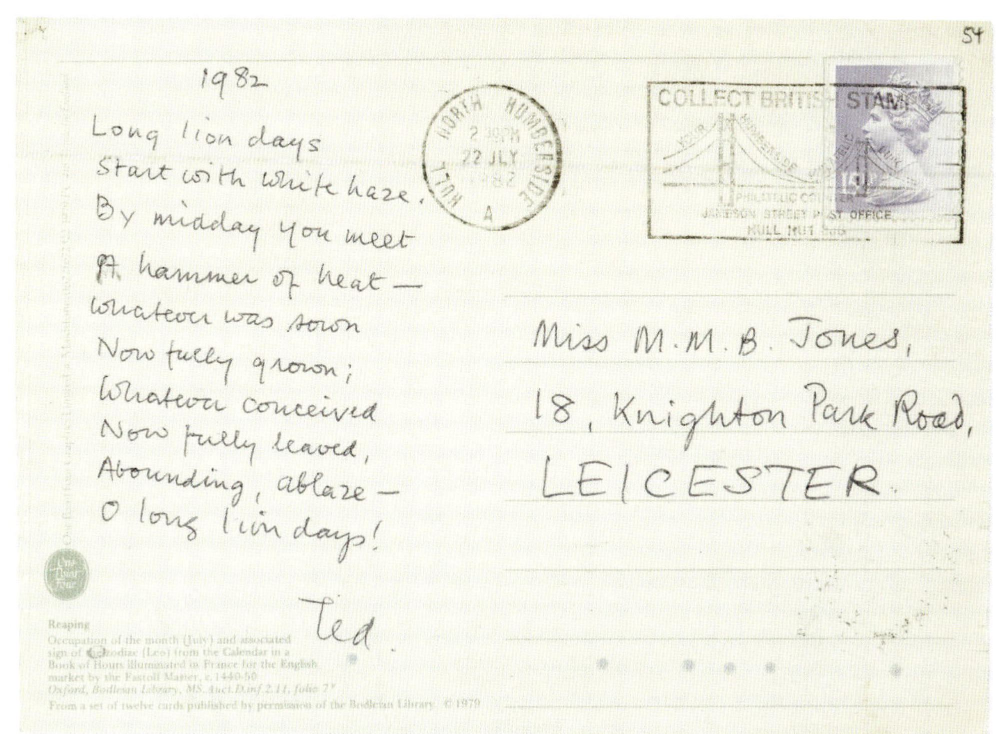
1982

Long lion days
Start with white haze.
By midday you meet
A hammer of heat –
Whatever was sown
Now fully grown;
Whatever conceived
Now fully leaved,
Abounding, ablaze –
O long lion days!

Ted

Miss M.M.B. Jones,
18, Knighton Park Road,
LEICESTER.

A strangely literal form of cutting is part of the relic business that was in vogue during and after the Romantic period. A hairlock of a 'genius' poet like Goethe, Shelley or Keats, especially if the genius had died young, was particularly coveted. John Keats was only twenty-five when he died of tuberculosis. He adored his fiancée and muse, Fanny Brawne, and gave her a lock of his hair towards the end of his life. She gave a portion of it to Keats's sister and it became a family heirloom, until a collector of Keats memorabilia set it in a ring (SEE FIG. 76). The ring was donated to the Bodleian in 1904.

There must have been more of these hairlocks of Keats in circulation. Around the time the hairlock ring was donated to the Bodleian, a big Keats fan made his own poetry from Keats's hair: the war poet Wilfred Owen (1893–1918) wrote a poem 'On Seeing a Lock of Keats' Hair', emulating Keats (SEE FIG. 77).[147]

He read all of Keats's poetry; tried to emulate Keats's style; annotated several books by Keats and read *Adonais*, Shelley's elegy on the death of Keats.

Owen's gesture of writing a poem 'On Seeing a Lock' was itself inspired by Keats, who in his turn had written a poem titled 'Lines on Seeing a Lock of Milton's Hair':

For many years my offerings must be hush'd:
When I do speak I'll think upon this hour,
Because I feel my forehead hot and flush'd,
Even at the simplest vassal of thy Power,–
A Lock of thy bright hair![148]

76 Lock of John Keats's hair, set in a ring (Oxford, Bodleian Library, MS. Cons. Res. Objects 65)

77 Manuscript of Wilfred Owen's poem 'On Seeing a Lock of Keats' Hair' (Oxford, Bodleian Library, Bodleian MS. 12282/2 (OEF 207)

Not unlike Keats, Owen had a 'tremendous capacity for admiration, for reverence', as his colleague Osbert Sitwell puts it.[149] And, like Keats, he sings out his excitement at seeing the lock, flagging it with an exclamation mark:

It is a lock of Adonais' hair!
I dare not look too long; nor try to tell
What glories I see glistening, glistening there.
The unanointed eye cannot perceive their spell.
Turn ye to Adonais; his great spirit seek.
O hear him; he will speak!

Owen was nineteen when he wrote his poem in 1912, seeking Keats's 'great spirit'. The manuscript makes almost palpable how Owen attempts to apply

① On seeing a lock of Keats Hair

Once ~~I remember seeing a~~ in a convent I beheld ~~a pallid~~ ~~scarlet~~ nun,
~~Who Kissed with adorant lips~~ With lips adorant Kiss a ~~the scarlet~~ dirty fringe
~~Some~~ Of ~~some~~ Pope's ~~had~~ vestment cast off ~~given her~~ ~~with his~~ changed with benison.
That ~~such~~ thus a spirit~~ual~~ ~~form~~ to such ~~base~~ stuff should cringe;
That ~~such a~~ guileless souls should so ~~itself~~ themselves beguile;
I smiled a pitiful smile.

②

~~And once I oversaw~~
~~Not long ago~~ And not long since, I caught a lover bland
Gazing ~~with~~ this ~~tearful eyes~~ tears upon a ~~little~~ silken glove,
Stolen, ~~perchance~~ I doubt not, from some ~~small~~ small shrinking hand.
That ~~such an~~ empty things should hold ~~so~~ ~~silke content~~ ~~great~~ plenteous a love,
~~Thant~~ That Passion's ~~hunger~~ could be fed ~~feedeth~~ on ~~such~~ that poor chaff. so fe[illegible]
I laughed a bitter laugh. { ~~that~~ That hungry passion could be fed on chaff.

③

But why this ~~at present~~ ~~moment~~ ~~day~~ moment does my ~~spirit~~ our soul heart cower,
And all ~~to~~ my faculties bow down with awe?
~~My~~ All ~~turn has~~ time is come to ~~feel~~ know a relic's power
I ~~feel~~ my ~~cheeks~~ brow mouth ~~with glowing anguish drawn~~ in with new, ~~unbitter~~ voluptuous anguish drawn
~~And I feel the dear[illegible]~~
~~And bless see this gift in the vast barrier of years~~
And ~~memory~~ ~~My hand is~~ My ~~being~~ ~~Now happy happy~~ with a terrible trouble ~~tears.~~ My ~~heart~~ ~~time terrible~~ ~~pulse~~ throbs
throbs ~~And all my~~ my sobs.
And ~~Keats~~ hearts ~~Hell~~ Hades

④

It is a lock of Adonais' hair!
I dare not look too long; nor try to tell
What glories I see glistening, glistening there
The unanointed eye can not perceive their spell.
~~But turn to him first who wore the~~
Turn ~~ye~~ to Adonais; his great spirit seek.
O hear him; he will speak!

the advice Keats once gave his friend Shelley: 'curb your magnanimity and be more of an artist and "load every rift" of your subject with ore'.[150] In his draft, Owen is filling every rift with loaded words, training himself to become a great poet. Which he did. Unfortunately also one who died young, at the age of twenty-five, like Keats. He died in battle, on 4 November 1918, only a week before the war came to an end. He will forever be remembered for his poems on the futility of war and on the lies with which people are lured into fighting for their country.

For his most famous poem, 'Dulce et decorum est', he cut a line from Horace's Ode III.2. He actually cut it in two, calling it 'the old lie'; the full line reads: 'Dulce et decorum est pro patria mori' (it is sweet and proper to die for one's country). The manuscripts are not as 'loaded' with substitutions as in 'On Seeing a Lock of Keats' Hair', but here every *word* is loaded, even the ones that did not make it into publication, such as the belching black blood, which becomes 'green' and 'thick' and 'gargling' in the next version (SEE FIG. 78):

> If you could see, ~~the~~ at every jolt, the blood
> Come belching black and frothy from the lung,
> And think ~~that~~ how once his face was like a bud,
> Fresh as a country rose, and clear, and young,
> You would not go on telling with such zest,
> To ~~youngsters~~ children ardent for some desperate glory,
> The old lie: Dulce et decorum est
> Pro patria mori.

The 'youngsters' were replaced by 'children'; in the next version they became 'small boys':

> If you could hear, at every jolt, the blood
> Come gargling ~~green~~ thick and frothy from the lung;
> And think how once his face was like a bud,
> Fresh as a country rose, and ~~light~~ keen, and young,
> You'd not go telling with such noble zest,
> To small boys, ardent ~~from~~ for some desperate glory,
> The old lie: Dulce et decorum est
> Pro patria mori.

But by the published version Owen decided 'children' was the most loaded word.

The manuscripts are written in a neat, legible hand. They almost look like fair copies. But following these versions, several textual casualties still occurred before the armistice of publication. The most notable casualties are the two lines of loveliness, where the memory of the young man's face is compared to a bud, 'clear' then 'light' then 'keen', fresh as a country rose – 'country' presaging the 'patria' in the last line. Even that faint memory of beauty and peace is not allowed to survive. The promising 'bud' is replaced by the revolting 'cud'. This revision is the wryest application of Q's principle: 'Murder your darlings'. It is Owen's bitter reply to the previous generation, the generation of Quiller-Couch, who – together with Colonel Dudley Acland Mills – had raised an entire battalion (the Duke of Cornwall's Light Infantry 10th Battalion or 'Cornwall Pioneers'), undoubtedly employing the old lie of *mori* for glory:

> If you could hear, at every jolt, the blood
> Come gargling from the froth-corrupted lungs,
> Obscene as cancer, bitter as the cud
> Of vile, incurable sores on innocent tongues, –
> My friend, you would not tell with such high zest
> To children ardent for some desperate glory,
> The old Lie: *Dulce et decorum est*
> *Pro patria mori.*[151]

OVERLEAF

78 Draft of Wilfred Owen's poem 'Dulce et decorum est' (Oxford, Bodleian Library, MS. 12282/4 (OEF 316–317)

Dulce et Decorum est.

(To Jessie Pope etc.)

~~Hunched~~ Bent, like old rag + bone men under sacks;
Knock-kneed; coughing like hags, we cursed through sludge.
Till on the glimmering flares we turned our backs,
And towards our distant rest began to trudge.
Halting each mile, for ~~many~~ some had lost their boots,
And limped on, blood-shod. All went lame; all blind;
Drunk with fatigue; deaf even to the hoots
Of disappointed shells that dropped behind.
Then somewhere near in front: Whew, fup, fop, fup-
Gas-shells or duds? We loosened masks in case -
And listened... Nothing... Far guns grumbled Krupp -
Then smartly Poison hit us in the face.
Gas! GAS! An ecstasy of fumbling,
Fitting the clumsy helmets, just in time.

P.T.O.

But someone still was yelling out, and stumbling,
And floundring like a man in fire or lime.
There, through the misty panes and dim green light,
As under a thick sea, I saw him drowning...

I must not speak of this thing as I might.
In all my dreams I ~~see~~ hear him choking, drowning.
In all your dreams if you could slowly pace
Behind the wagon that we laid him in,
And watch the white eyes turning in his face,
His hanging face, tortured for your own sin, —
If you could see, ~~the~~ at every jolt, the blood
Come belching black and frothy from the lung,
And think ~~that~~ how once his face was like a bud,
Fresh as a country rose, and clear, and young,
You would not go on telling with such zest,
To ~~[illegible]~~ children ardent for some desperate glory,
The old lie : Dulce et decorum est
Pro patria mori.

Oct. 8. 1917

~~[illegible] to support —~~

~~“Your Eyes are a Compliment to your [illegible] my Lord, said Emma bowing, tho' I do not exactly understand it.” Lord Osborne laughed rather awkwardly, & then said “Upon my soul, I am a bad hand at Compliments. [illegible] I believe you [illegible] & after some minutes silence, added, “Can you give me a better hint without offering [illegible] Compt. I should be very glad to learn.” “I could [illegible] could not say a syllable [illegible] repressed his [illegible] freedom of his manner. He had too much sense not to take the hint — & when he spoke again, it was with a degree of [illegible] propriety which he had never used before. [illegible]~~ employing [illegible]

by a gracious answer, & a more full view of her face than she had yet bestowed. ~~[illegible]~~ Unused to exert himself, & happy in contem:plating her, he sat in silence for ~~about five~~ then some minutes longer, while Tom Musgrave was chatter:ing to Elizth, till they were interrupted by Nanny's half [illegible] the door & putting

10

CUTS IN BORN-DIGITAL WORKS

Birthmark / Silver — hallmark —

On my decline, a millipede
Helped me to keep count;
For every time I slipped a foot
Further down ~~the~~ life's mountain

He'd leave a tiny, cast-off limb
Of crimson on my cheek,
As if to say –
You're hurting us both, Mick...

This thousandth morning after, though,
I miss his prickly touch, ~~tread~~
And scrubbing at the mirror
~~I don't like much~~ / find instead
Instead of a thousand scratches
~~The~~ a big new blue birthmark ~~splashed~~ stamped
From ear to bilberry ear, —
His whole body of blood's
~~Inky smear~~ Untimely smear.

He must have had no more to give
Of warnings, ~~being dismembered so,~~
But had to stain me with his death
~~That all might know~~ ~~And not this is:~~
~~In case we forgot~~ Lest we forget
~~It is~~ That it's as bad to fall astray
As to start from the wrong place.
Now I have earned the purple face
It won't go away.

~~And to my~~
And so I had a complexion
Like many another drinker
Whose colour was less pink
Than gradually pinker
mirror — ~~ren~~ memento mori

And so by small degrees
~~Graduation~~ pink...

murray mint

And so we lost our legs together
(mine temporarily)
But I ~~saw him more~~ never thought what the mirror meant
~~Than~~ was a memento mori.

turning to

But what I thought the mirror meant
As we lost our legs together
(Mine temporarily)
Than a memento mori

a badge for life
Than a memento mori

with his legs
with his legs all shot
~~with his legs all in~~
in a sense
/ gone.
Remembered innocence
Remembered

preach

~~I~~ thought the
~~Than~~ the mirror meant more

Since we have so many traces of cuts in 'analogue' literature, the big question is whether there will be any vestiges of 'born-digital' works. Many of us just overwrite earlier versions of a text we are working on. If we write an email – even if we use, say, the 'Drafts' function in Outlook – we do, we undo and we redo, in Louise Bourgeois' words (see Chapter 1), but we redo by erasing the earlier version. Similarly, poets write poetry on their smartphones, one of the most ephemeral media. But the question is also: does that really differ so much from the analogue situation? Take the case of Jane Austen. We do have quite a few traces of her writing, but we do not have any traces of some of her most loved works, such as *Pride and Prejudice*. In her analogue time there was only one physical copy; once it was sent to the publisher it was out of her hands. Suppose she had written her work on a computer, and suppose – like most of us – she overwrote her earlier versions. Even then she would have had to send a version to the publisher at some point. She would probably have kept that version on her hard drive. That would already have been more of a trace than we have now. If she had sent her manuscript as an attachment to an email and copied in an extra person at the publisher's, the version would have been distributed to two people. Even if one of them would have deleted it, the other one might have kept it. That is a 'reasonable percentage', as Vladimir puts it in Beckett's *Waiting for Godot*. The editor would have worked on it, made suggestions and sent it back to the author. Or, even if they did not, they would have sent it to the printer. In terms of distribution, the situation of digital manuscripts thus starts resembling the situation of medieval manuscripts, where the rule is: the more a work is copied, the higher its chances of survival. And even if we focus solely on the private space of the author's personal computer, it is possible to retrieve a lot of data by means

LEFT & FOLLOWING PAGES

79 Drafts of Mick Imlah's poem 'Birthmark' (Oxford, Bodleian Library, MS. 12919/1, Folder 2)

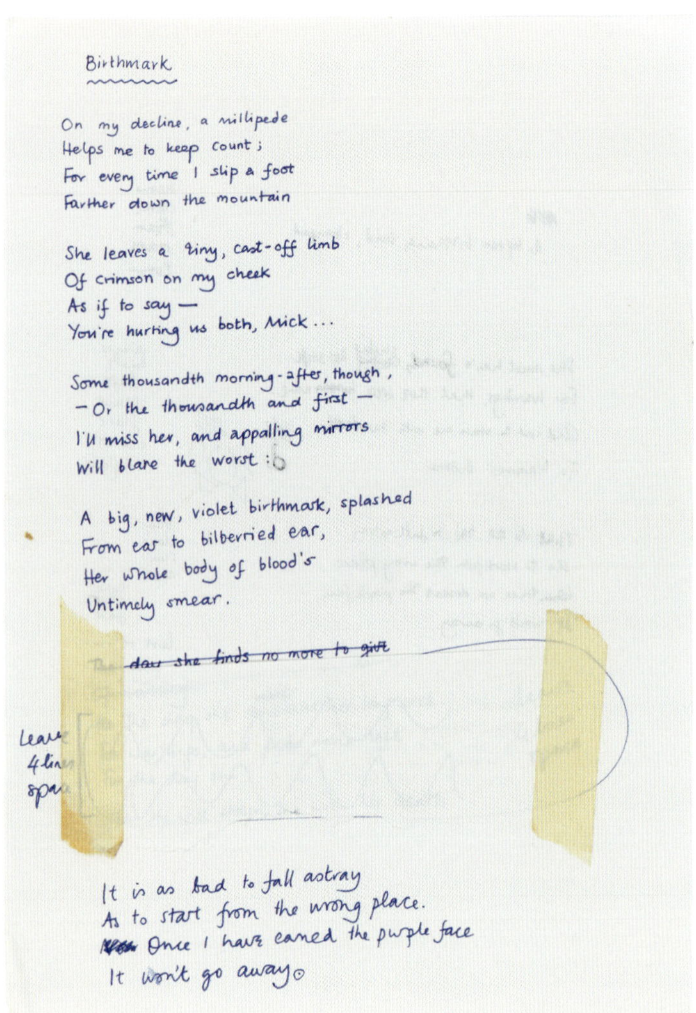
Birthmark

On my decline, a millipede
Helps me to keep count;
For every time I slip a foot
Farther down the mountain

She leaves a tiny, cast-off limb
Of crimson on my cheek
As if to say —
You're hurting us both, Mick ...

Some thousandth morning-after, though,
— Or the thousandth and first —
I'll miss her, and appalling mirrors
Will blare the worst:

A big, new, violet birthmark, splashed
From ear to bilberried ear,
Her whole body of blood's
Untimely smear.

~~The day she finds no more to give~~

It is as bad to fall astray
As to start from the wrong place.
Once I have earned the purple face
It won't go away.

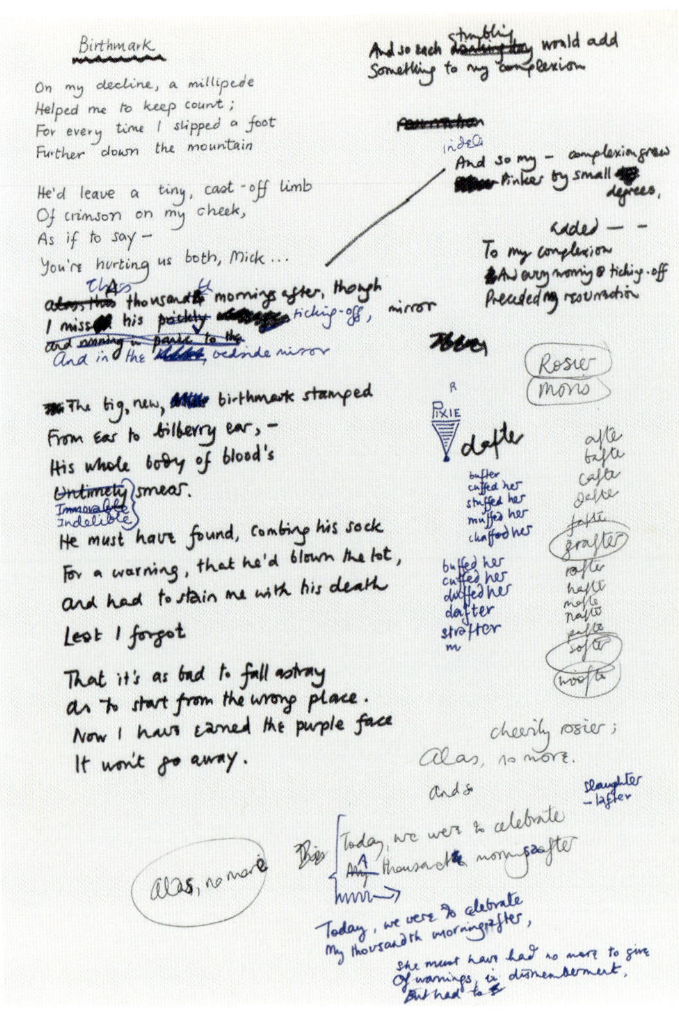
Birthmark

On my decline, a millipede
Helped me to keep count;
For every time I slipped a foot
Further down the mountain

He'd leave a tiny, cast-off limb
Of crimson on my cheek,
As if to say —
You're hurting us both, Mick ...

The big, new, birthmark stamped
From ear to bilberry ear, —
His whole body of blood's
Untimely smear.
He must have found, combing his sock
For a warning, that he'd blown the lot,
and had to stain me with his death
Lest I forgot

That it's as bad to fall astray
As to start from the wrong place.
Now I have earned the purple face
It won't go away.

of digital forensics – which is what was applied to Salman Rushdie's personal computer, held at Emory University.[152]

To explore how cuts play a role in born-digital works it is useful to start from an analogue example: the genesis of a poem by the British poet Mick Imlah (1956–2009). The main theme linking the poems of his collection of poetry *Birthmarks* is that there are always 'things – class, family, congenital strengths and weaknesses, prejudices, addictions, tattoos, that people are stuck with, whether they like it or not'.[153] One of the poems in the collection is titled 'Birthmark' (singular). It suggests that people can also pick up such fixed marks or burdens along the way, in their lifetime. More than half a dozen handwritten versions of this poem are kept in the Bodleian's Special Collections (SEE FIG. 79).[154]

If you put them all next to each other, they resemble a storyboard, a sequence of drawings representing the shots planned for a film production. Together, they tell the story of all the things Imlah had to cut and revise to arrive at the version he deemed ready for publication. When scholars make a transcript of a version, they can transcribe everything they find on the page that belongs to this particular poem, and present it either in a 'topographic' way (respecting the place of every word as they find it on the page) or in a 'linearized' way (putting the words in the right sequence). The first method focuses on what you see (the document as an image); the second method puts the emphasis on making it readable (the document as a text).

In some traditions, however, such as 'authorial philology' in Italy or the layer-by-layer method in Russian 'textology', scholars try to reconstruct

Birthmark

On my decline, a millipede
Helped me to keep count;
For every time I slipped a foot
Further down the mountain

He'd leave a tiny, cast-off limb
Of crimson on my cheek
As if to say –
You're hurting us both, Mick...

This thousandth morning after, though,
I miss his prickly touch,
And scrubbing at the mirror
I don't like much

The big new blue birthmark splashed
From ear to bilberry ear, –
His whole body of blood's
Inky smear.

He must have had no more to give
Of warnings, being dismembered so,
But had to stain me with his death
That all might know

It is as bad to fall astray
As to start from the wrong place.
Now I have earned the purple face
It won't go away.

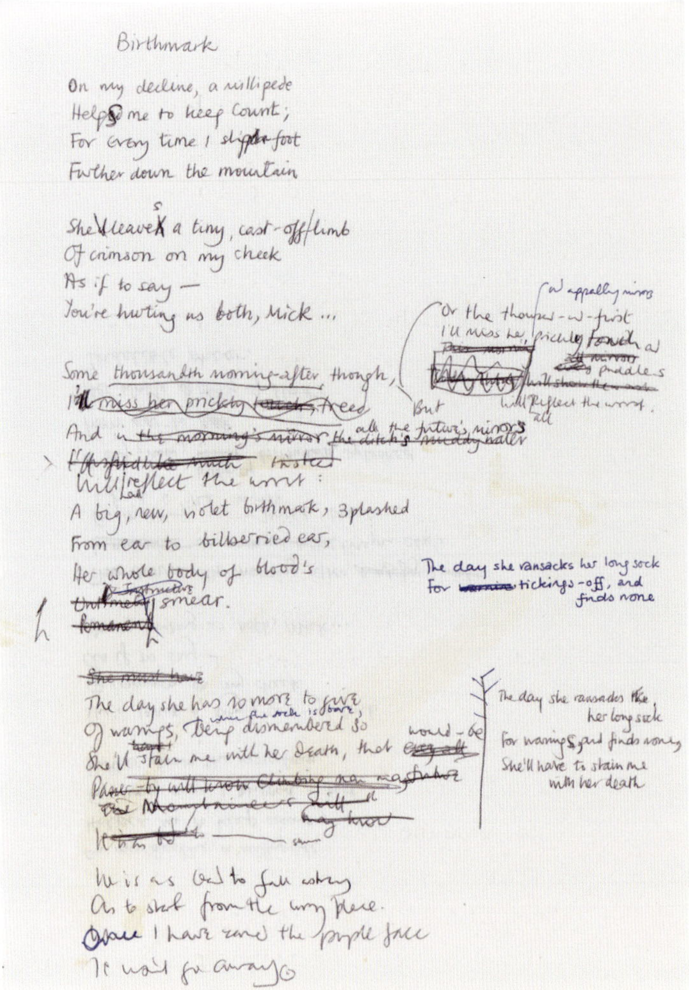

Birthmark

On my decline, a millipede
Helps me to keep count;
For every time I slip a foot
Further down the mountain

She leaves a tiny, cast-off limb
Of crimson on my cheek
As if to say –
You're hurting us both, Mick...

Some thousandth morning-after though,
will reflect the worst:
A big, new, violet birthmark, splashed
From ear to bilberried ear,
Her whole body of blood's
smear.

The day she ransacks her long sock
For tickings-off, and finds none

The day she has no more to give
Of warnings, being dismembered so
She'll stain me with her death, that

It is as bad to fall astray
As to start from the wrong place.
Once I have earned the purple face
It won't go away.

the sequence of writing within one document. Some authors make use of a different writing tool whenever they revise their text. For instance, as we saw in Chapter 4, Raymond Chandler's typescript of *The Long Good-bye* ended with a typed layer, followed by additions in respectively red and blue ballpoint pen. In such a case, it would be possible to discern a writing sequence of, say, first the black text, then the red revisions, then the blue ones. If it works to transcribe the text layer by layer, the story of the genesis becomes more refined, and instead of a succession of images, as in a storyboard, the transcriptions start coming closer to the movie of the genesis.

That is what Russian scholars in the twentieth century made: a movie of Pushkin's poem 'The Bronze Horseman' in the making (1937). After the 1937 film, a new one was made in 1961 (SEE FIGS 80 & 81). They reconstructed word by word how Pushkin made each revision.[155] Of course, if all that is left is a sheet of paper with traces of writing in black ink, and if all the corrections and revisions have been made in the same black ink, it can be quite hard to reconstruct the writing sequence. Often, the reconstruction will be so speculative and require so much interpretation that no two colleagues would come up with exactly the same reconstruction.

But imagine Pushkin were living now, writing his poem on a smartphone. Or suppose Jane Austen wrote *Pride and Prejudice* on a laptop and she had installed a keystroke-logging software programme on her computer, registering every key she struck on her keyboard, every pause, every typo, every idea that was only half-developed but then abandoned, every road not taken. There would be a record of all the cuts, and it would be possible to 'replay' the recorded data.

Imagine the opening sentence of *Pride and Prejudice* had not always been the bold statement that has become so famous: 'It is a truth universally acknowledged, that a single man in possession of a good fortune, must be in want of a wife.' Suppose Jane Austen initially started with 'This is a universal truth', then changed it to a provocative platitude like 'It is a truth universally acknowledged that a single woman must be in want of a husband', and only then changed a single 'woman' into a single 'man', more specifically a 'man in possession of a good fortune', and a 'husband' into a 'wife'.[156] During that process, she would also inevitably pause here and there, make a few typos and immediately correct them. All these actions would be replayable. Instead of a facsimile image of a page full of deletions and substitutions, we would have a 'dynamic facsimile'. Since this 'writing footage' also captures pauses, it enables the study of phenomena such as 'fluency' or 'writer's block'.

This may seem very intrusive, but there are several writers who take this initiative themselves – for various reasons. The British author Craig M. Taylor wrote his novel *Staying On* (2018)

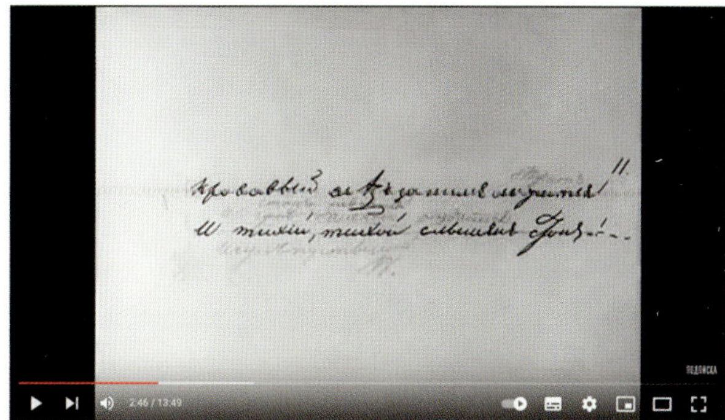

Рукописи Пушкина А.С. (1937)

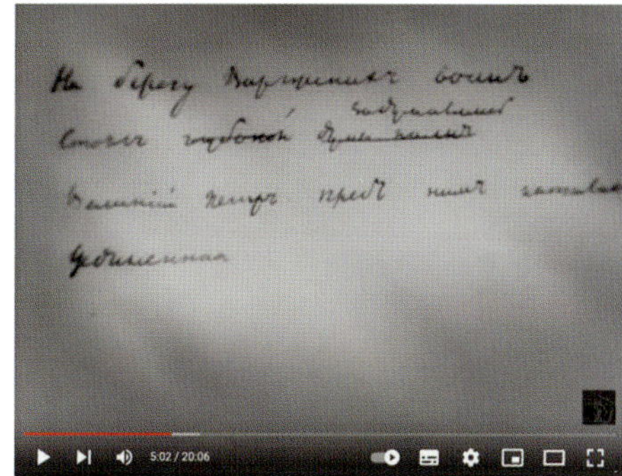

Рукописи Пушкина / 1961

80 Reconstruction of the writing process of Pushkin's poem 'The Bronze Horsman', 1937 version. YouTube (www.youtube.com/watch?v=_IJjyzvg1Uo)

81 Reconstruction of the writing process of Pushkin's poem 'The Bronze Horsman', 1961 version. YouTube (www.youtube.com/watch?v=f5FHyn9F7eo)

in collaboration with the British Library, documenting the entire four-year writing process with keystroke-logging software. What is often seen as an invasion of an intimate creative space (the installation of a form of spyware on the writer's computer) became a request. Taylor even explained in a blog post why he contacted the British Library before starting his book project. He was concerned, on the one hand, about the perceived loss of drafts in born-digital works, and, on the other hand, about 'the long-haul loneliness of novel writing, a process I considered in my most despairing moment as like wallpapering a dungeon'.[157] In that sense it had a motivating effect. According to Taylor, 'it actually did help me begin again with novel writing'. Instead of feeling spied upon, he experienced the keystroke logging as a form of collaboration: 'Somehow the writing felt collaborative, not only because the software was recording me, but also because of the digital curation team who were taking the data.'[158]

In this way the writing process increasingly becomes part of the novel. And this connection between process and product is not limited to novel writing, but also applies to other genres, such as poetry. An online journal titled *Midst* publishes poems as products, including the process of their making. The key question that drives the enterprise is: 'What if you could watch your favourite poet write?' (SEE FIG. 82).

The journal has existed since 2019, and is run by poet and designer Annelyse Gelman and software developer Jason Gillis-Grier. They present their journal as a platform to share poems 'in the form of interactive timelapses': 'You'll see the finished text by default, but then you can rewind it to see exactly how it was written: start to finish, blank page to final draft, and every edit in between.'[159]

A particularly illustrative example of how this 'work-in-progress' presentation reveals the art of cutting is Franny Choi's poem 'Cuttings' (SEE FIG. 83). The start button prompts a screen that shows that the very first letters the poet typed were just the central keys on the keyboard for both the right and the left hand – 'lkjsdlf' (FIG. 84).

This finger exercise was followed by a space and then the letters 'jasdf'. The random letter combination 'ja' seems to have triggered the word 'january': Choi deleted all she had written so far and typed 'january'. The next step was a combination of words: 'january fever dreams with organ'; 'organ' may have been a typo; it was immediately replaced by 'oranges'; and then the text

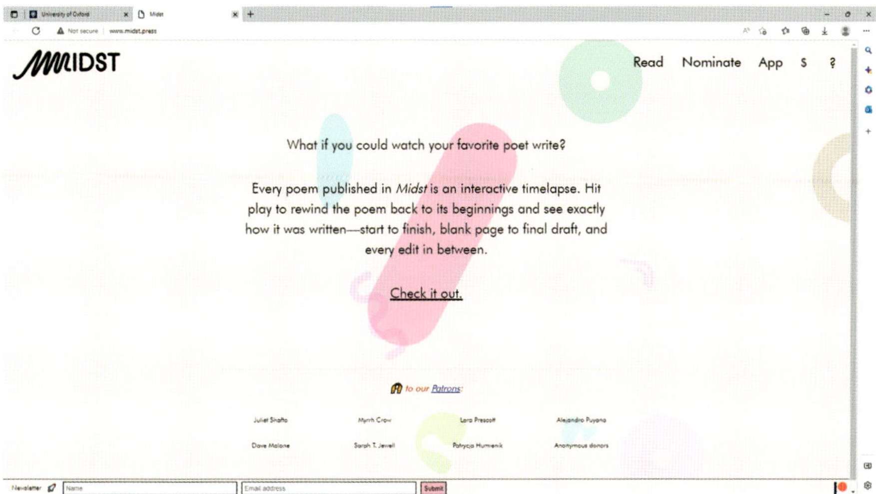

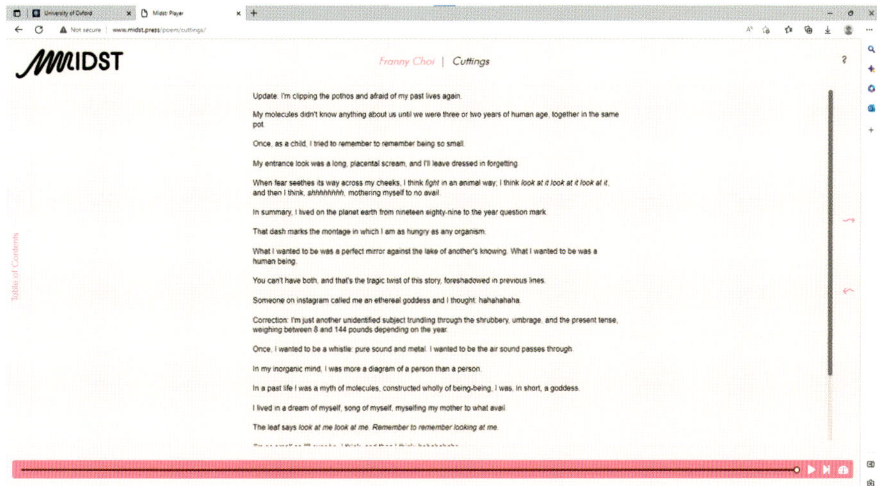

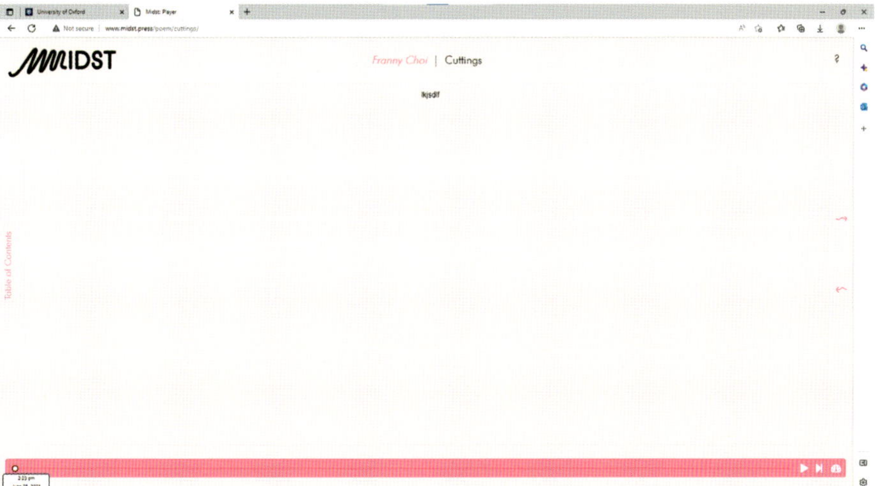

82 Screenshot of the online journal *Midst*, homepage, 14 January 2023 (www.midst.press)

83 Final version of Franny Choi's 'Cuttings', screenshot of the online journal *Midst*, 14 January 2023 (www.midst.press)

84 Earliest stage of the writing process of Franny Choi's 'Cuttings', screenshot of the online journal *Midst*, 14 January 2023 (www.midst.press)

continued, 'slipping through my fingers'. Choi continued writing in what appears to be one continuous block of text, not caring too much about spelling at this point just yet. For instance:

> if i lived and there'sno afterlife to hear it does it make a difference. does it mean it happened. i lived here on the planet earth from nineteen eighty nine to hte year question mark.

Since the journal's keystroke logging software does not show the length of pauses, the text seems to grow steadily until it reads:

> i'm not made for this world, you say, and so i imagine a better one. i imagine the kind that loves us the way we deserve. i imagine one that sings about people as if we are them.

At that moment (25 June 2021, 3.46 p.m.) Choi starts rereading and revising the text produced so far. That is when 'there'sno afterlife' and 'hte year' are corrected (3.49 p.m.). The preliminary end of the block of text is also revised. Choi cuts 'so i imagine a better one. i imagine the kind that loves us the way we deserve. i imagine one that sings about people as if we are them.' And she changes it to: 'i'm not made for this world, you say, and if that's a reason to imagine a better one, that's what I'll do' (25 June 2021, 3.54 p.m.). At that moment Choi decides to cut the first 92 words of the 540 words produced so far:

> january fever dreams with oranges slipping through my fingers, you ran through me like that. sordid as a year, as showerless, as hungry as an actual human organ wondering at its demise. it was me all along, wondering. it was true, what i said, that the unable of death its un-possible its ex-be, that was the most frightening thing. that was the worst plot hole. it wasn't true, what i said, that the years below this one were blinking in response to us. our foreign organicity. our slapering, singular splice. another morning

At the next stage, the block of text is cut into shorter lines by means of hard returns. For instance, Choi cuts the line 'if i lived and there'sno afterlife to hear it does it make a difference. does it mean it happened.' It is replaced by 'in summary':

> in summary, i lived on the planet earth
> from nineteen eighty nine to the year question mark.

The hard return is immediately reconsidered and placed elsewhere:

> in summary, i lived on the planet earth from nineteen
> eighty nine to the year question mark.
>
> (3.59 p.m.)

And that is the moment Choi comes up with a metaphor of montage, adding first 'along that dash is me' and then 'along that dash is a montage of me':

> in summary, i lived on the planet earth from nineteen
> eighty nine to the year question mark. along that dash is a montage of me
>
> (4.00 p.m.)

In the next revision campaign, Choi starts adding more space between the lines:

> in summary, i lived on the planet earth from nineteen eighty nine to the year question mark.
>
> that dash marks the montage of me in which i am as hungry as any organic being.
>
> (4.02 p.m.)

At 4.15 p.m., all the lower-case first-person pronouns (as in 'i lived') are replaced by capitals. The first time a title appears is at 4.19–4.20 p.m. (25 June 2021): 'PROPAGATION'. Then nothing happened for nine minutes, until the title is replaced by 'CUTTINGS' (4.29 p.m.).

That was the last writing act of that day's productive session. The next writing session was five days later, 30 June 2021, at half past eight in the evening. One of the things that changed at this stage was that the 'organic being' (which in the meantime had already been changed into an 'organic creature') now became an 'organism'. The poem appears to have been left to rest for almost half a year. After a very short, two-minute session on 8 December at 1.00 a.m. the poem was finished – with another interval of a few months – on 14 February 2022, shortly after 9.00 a.m. Especially given the metaphor of the dash marking 'the montage of me' it is remarkable that one of the very last changes Choi made to her poem was a dash-like finishing touch, the addition of a hyphen in 'eighty-nine': 'In summary, I lived on the planet earth from nineteen eighty-nine to the year question mark.'

~~CONCLUSION~~
THE CUTTING-ROOM FLOOR

In the spirit of this book, we cut the conclusion, and present the cutting-room floor instead. All the unused footage that did not make it into the film is lying here scattered on the floor. For instance, there was no space for a discussion of *Agrippa (a book of the dead)*, which appeared in 1992 as a collaboration between artist Dennis Ashbaugh, author William Gibson and publisher Kevin Begos Jr. This book contains a 3½-inch diskette with a 'self-destructive' poem by Gibson that was conceived not just as a born-digital but also as a die-digital work: the reader could run the text of the poem, scrolling up the screen, but in the meantime an encryption program on the diskette encoded each line and made the poem disappear after its first reading.[160] So the poem 'cut' itself, as it were, as soon as the reader read it.

The cutting-room floor reminds us of the necessity of cutting as an essential part of telling a story. That also applies to this book, which has a paradoxical relation to its topic. On the one hand, drawing attention to a few scenes that were cut is not the same as offering the 'director's cut'. All we have been able to do is offer the elements with which readers can imaginatively reconstruct the 'uncut version'. On the other hand, it would not be right to present this book as the humble work of simply sampling or sweeping the cutting-room floor of literature. Retracing the genesis of a literary work requires its own fair share of cutting. When you start telling these stories of cutting, you inevitably have to prune and curate as well. The story of the genesis is never objective; it is also a narrative. And for every narrative, professionals such as Q, William Faulkner or Stephen King seem to be unanimous in their advice: 'Kill your darlings'. Or, as Ford Madox Ford told Jean Rhys: 'When in doubt, cut.'[161]

Even at this very moment, more cuts by contemporary authors are whirling onto the cutting-room floor. Alice Oswald, for instance, often starts writing a poem by means of a drawing, which gradually gives way to words. As the first female poet to hold the post of Professor of Poetry at the University of Oxford in its 300-year history, she dedicated her inaugural lecture to the Art of Erosion, 'mostly to adjust the balance between the livingness and the lastingness of poetry': 'We tend to assume that the good poems are the ones that last, but of course poems also need to live and one of the requirements of living is dying, i.e. vanishing.'[162] Oswald distinguishes 'constructed poems' from 'eroded poems' and holds a plea for 'poets of erosion because their task is not so much to fortify or decorate the language as to wear some holes in it', referring to Samuel Beckett's description of Beethoven's music as a 'tonal surface, eaten into by large black pauses'. The reference is taken from a letter he wrote to a German friend – in German – describing his developing poetics in terms of boring holes into his language and wondering whether there was any reason 'why that terribly arbitrary materiality of the word's surface should not be dissolved'.[163] One way of achieving this 'literature of the unword' (*Literatur des Unworts*) was by cutting rather than appending, decomposing rather than composing, subtracting rather than adding, eroding rather than constructing. The art of erosion is typically a process, to which the cuts on the cutting-room floor attest; and it remains a process, even when one reads the so-called finished product. For, as Alice Oswald puts it, 'a poem isn't always what happens in the words but is the trace that the words leave inside you as it vanishes.'[164]

I Keep an iris in a jar

[illegible] afterbirth [illegible]

[illegible] the bright [illegible]

Raisins

JOB

Through Wordsworth's Lamps.

To a withered hand

Clinging as a

Last Straw

Will these break a
straw drawn back & fro?

Leaf

ALICE OSWALD

AFTERWORD

A SHORT POEM IS MADE mostly by cutting phrases from an imagined long poem – and among the bits discarded there are often mere swirls and colours, like the ones shown here. These abstract sketches represent first attempts to catch a feeling in my head, to which I subsequently attach phrases – like finding a musical score before you can read music. I try to erase all this from my mind afterwards and am deliberately careless with notebooks, in order that unfinished workings don't haunt future poems; so I can't completely remember the workings on display here. I think they were all stages in a slow-built poem about an Iris, which I kept in a jam jar for several years watching the process of its withering and vanishing… A finished poem was published with a series of photographs of a fading petal by Garry Fabian Miller, in a pamphlet titled *Cyanometer: instruments for measuring blueness* (The Letter Press, 2023).

85 Sketches from Alice Oswald's notebooks

NOTES

1. Stephen King, *On Writing: A Memoir of the Craft*, Scribner, New York, 2000, p. 222.
2. Sir Arthur Quiller-Couch, *On the Art of Writing: Lectures Delivered in the University of Cambridge 1913–1914*, Cambridge at the University Press, 1920, ch. 12 'On Style'. The manuscript is kept at the library of Trinity College, Oxford. We owe a debt of gratitude to Clare Hopkins and Claire Qu for drawing our attention to Q's manuscripts.
3. Bruno Latour, *Pandora's Hope: Essays on the Reality of Science Studies*, Harvard University Press, Cambridge MA, 1999, pp. 179–80.
4. Severin Fowles, 'People Without Things', in Mikkel Bille, Frida Hastrup and Tim Flohr Sørensen (eds), *An Anthropology of Absence: Materializations of Transcendence and Loss*, Springer, New York, 2010, pp. 23–41.
5. Bodleian Library MS. Eng. poet. C. 1, fol. 01v.
6. Robert M. Schmitz, *Pope's 'Essay on Criticism' 1709: A Study of the Bodleian Manuscript Text with Facsimiles, Transcripts, and Variants*, Washington University Press, St Louis MS, 1962, p. 9.
7. Alexander Pope, *The Works of Alexander Pope Esq. in Nine Volumes Complete, with his last Corrections, Additions, and Improvements*, ed. M. Warburton, Knapton, Lintot, Tonson, and Draper, London, 1751, p. 90.
8. Bodleian Library MS. Eng. poet. C. 1, fol. 03r.
9. Samuel Beckett, 'Sottisier' Notebook, Beckett International Foundation, University of Reading, UoR MS 2901, fol. 15v.
10. James Knowlson, *Damned to Fame: The Life of Samuel Beckett*, Bloomsbury, London, 1996.
11. Alexander Pope, *An Essay on Criticism*, ed. John Sargeaunt, Clarendon Press, Oxford, 1909, p. 27. The book is part of Samuel Beckett's personal library. See the *Beckett Digital Library*, ed. Dirk Van Hulle, Mark Nixon and Vincent Neyt, www.beckettarchive.org/library/POP-ESS.html.
12. 'I Do, I Undo, I Redo' by Louise Joséphine Bourgeois (2000) is a work of art consisting of three steel towers, the first special commission for Tate Modern's Turbine Hall. Finn Fordham applied its title to literary writing processes. Finn Fordham, *I Do, I Undo, I Redo: The Textual Genesis of Modernist Selves in Hopkins, Yeats, Conrad, Forster, Joyce, and Woolf*, Oxford University Press, Oxford, 2010.
13. Christina Rossetti's poetry notebooks, Bodleian Library MS. Don. e. 1/1–9.
14. W.H. Auden, Bodleian MS. Eng. poet. c. 68.
15. Edward Thomas, Bodleian MS. Don. d. 28.
16. Bodleian MS. Eng. poet. e. 90. We owe a debt of gratitude to James Jackson for drawing our attention to this fascinating document.
17. Robert Bernard Martin, *Gerard Manley Hopkins: A Very Private Life*, G.P. Putnam's Sons, New York, 1991, p. 80.
18. Bodleian MS. Eng. e. 3764, quire 7, fol. 04r. See also Kathryn Sutherland, *Jane Austen's Textual Lives*, Oxford University Press, Oxford, 2005.

19. Bodleian MS. Eng. e. 3764, quire 7, fol. 04v.
20. UoR MS 2937/1, fol. 02r; quoted in Dirk Van Hulle, *Manuscript Genetics: Joyce's Know-How, Beckett's Nohow*, University of Florida Press, Gainesville FL, 2008, p. 160.
21. Mark Nixon, 'Beckett's Unpublished Canon', in S.E. Gontarski (ed.), *The Edinburgh Companion to Samuel Beckett and the Arts*, Edinburgh University Press, Edinburgh, 2014, p. 298.
22. Jenny Joseph, Bodleian MS. 12404/41.
23. Jenny Joseph, *Selected Poems*, Bloodaxe Books, Newcastle-upon-Tyne, 1999, p. 42.
24. Catherine McIlwaine dates the manuscript to May 1944 (personal correspondence, 22 August 2022).
25. We owe a debt of gratitude to Catherine McIlwaine for drawing our attention to this manuscript and noting that Tolkien in fact changed the topography at this point, and the two sketches on this page were probably part of his attempt to bring the story and the topography into harmony. Christopher Tolkien transcribes this page in J.R.R. Tolkien, *The War of the Ring*, vol. 8 of *History of Middle-earth*, Unwin Hyman, London, 1990. See pp. 183ff. for Christopher Tolkien's analysis of this draft.
26. J.R.R. Tolkien, Bodleian MS. Tolkien Drawings 81.
27. The last part of the text on the page characterizes Frodo and Sam respectively: 'Frodo went forward now – the last lap – and he exerted all his strength. He felt that if once he could get to the saddle of the pass and look over into the Nameless Land he would have accomplished something. Sam followed. He sensed evil all around him. He knew that they had walked into some trap, but what? He had sheathed his sword, but now he drew it in readiness. He halted for a moment, and stooped to pick up his staff with his left hand.'
28. J.R.R. Tolkien, *The Lord of the Rings*, Part Two: *The Two Towers*, HarperCollins, London, 1993, p. 405.
29. Ludwig Wittgenstein, pencil draft of *Tractatus Logico-Philosophicus,* Bodleian MS. German d. 6.
30. Ludwig Wittgenstein, carbon copy of *Tractatus Logico-Philosophicus,* Bodleian MS. German d. 7.
31. The 'false start' is written as a third-person narration with an innkeeper welcoming his guest; 'Der Wirt begrüsste den Gast', in Franz Kafka, *Das Schloss: Historisch-kritische Ausgabe sämtlicher Handschriften, Drucke und Typoskripte*, vol. 1, ed. Roland Reuss and Peter Staengle, Stroemfeld/Roter Stern, Frankfurt, 2018, pp. 4–5; MS. Kafka 34, fol. 01r.
32. Kafka, *Das Schloss*, vol. 1, pp. 10–11; MS. Kafka 34, fol. 02v. Above the short dividing line, Max Brod has pencilled: 'Hier beginnt der Roman „Das Schloss".'
33. Kafka, *Das Schloss*, vol. 1, pp. 80–81; MS. Kafka 34, fol. 20r.
34. Dorrit Cohn, 'K. Enters *The Castle*: On the Change of Person in Kafka's Manuscript', *Euphorion* 62, 1968, p. 32.
35. Kafka, *Das Schloss*, vol. 1, pp. 80–81; MS. Kafka 34, fol. 25r.
36. Kenneth Grahame, Bodleian MS. Eng. misc. e. 281, fols 01v–02r.
37. Q's manuscripts, lecture xii, 'On Style', Trinity College Library, Oxford.
38. Kenneth Grahame, Bodleian MS. Eng. misc. e. 247, fol. 09r.
39. Peter Hunt, *The Making of 'The Wind in the Willows'*, Bodleian Library Publishing, Oxford, 2018, p. 77.
40. Ibid., p. 9.
41. It is possible that the roots of *Excellent Women* reach even further back in time. In *The Life and Work of Barbara Pym*, Janice Rossen suggests that Pym's unpublished novella 'Something to Remember' (1940; Bodleian MS. Pym 11) 'must have been an early experiment for Excellent Women' (159). In 1950 Pym wrote an adaptation of 'Something to Remember', turning it into a radio play for the BBC (Bodleian MS. Pym 96).
42. Bodleian MS. Pym 14, fol. 02r.
43. Bodleian MS. Pym 14, fol. 01v.

44. This passage corresponds with Barbara Pym, *Excellent Women*, Little, Brown Book Group, London, 2022 (1952), p. 9.
45. Paula Byrne, *The Adventures of Miss Barbara Pym*, William Collins, London, 2022, p. 362.
46. Pym, *Excellent Women*, p. 9.
47. Bodleian MS. Eng. c. 2718, fol. 02r.
48. Bodleian MS. Eng. C. 7801 = SC 159.
49. Paul Muldoon, *The End of the Poem: Oxford Lectures*, Faber & Faber, London, 2009, p. 8.
50. Ibid..
51. Ibid.
52. Bodleian Library, Arch. AA. e. 97.
53. Ibid.
54. Bodleian Library, MS. Eng. d. 3978.
55. Bodleian Library, MS. Eng. c. 7801 = SC 159.
56. Quoted in Knowlson, *Damned to Fame*, p. 352.
57. Ibid.
58. John McNeill, *Something New Under the Sun: An Environmental History of the Twentieth-Century World*, W.W. Norton, New York, 2000, p. xxii.
59. Samuel Beckett, *Murphy*, ed. J.C.C. Mays, Faber & Faber, London, 2009, p. 3.
60. Samuel Beckett, manuscript of *Murphy*, University of Reading, UoR MS5517/1, 01r. This, and subsequent quotations from this manuscript, quoted in Dirk Van Hulle and Mark Nixon, *The Making of* Murphy, University Press Antwerp, Brussels, 2024.
61. UoR MS5517/1, 7v–8r.
62. Samuel Beckett, 'Notes on *Faust*', Beckett International Foundation, University of Reading, UoR MS 5004, 61; quoted in Dirk Van Hulle, 'Samuel Beckett's *Faust* Notes', *Samuel Beckett Today / Aujourd'hui* 16, 2006, p. 296.
63. Samuel Beckett, letter to Thomas MacGreevy, 19 August 1936, in *The Letters of Samuel Beckett*, Volume 1: *1929–1940*, ed. Martha Fehsenfeld and Lois More Overbeck, Cambridge University Press, Cambridge, 2009, p. 368.
64. Quoted in Van Hulle, 'Samuel Beckett's *Faust* Notes', p. 296.
65. Samuel Beckett, letter to George Reavey, 13 November 1936, in *The Letters of Samuel Beckett, vol. 1,* p. 380.
66. Beckett, letter to George Reavey, 20 December 1936, in *The Letters of Samuel Beckett*, vol. 1, p. 399.
67. Beckett, letter to Thomas MacGreevy, 9 September 1936, in *The Letters of Samuel Beckett*, vol. 1, p. 371 n3.
68. Beckett, letter to Thomas MacGreevy, 19 September 1936, in *The Letters of Samuel Beckett*, vol. 1, *p.* 370.
69. Beckett, letter to Thomas MacGreevy, 9 October 1936, in *The Letters of Samuel Beckett*, vol. 1, p. 376.
70. Samuel Beckett, 'Whoroscope' Notebook, Beckett International Foundation, University of Reading, UoR MS 3000, fol. 34r; quoted in Samuel Beckett, *The Collected Poems of Samuel Beckett*, ed. Seán Lawlor and John Pilling, Faber & Faber, London, 2012, p. 366.
71. Samuel Beckett, 'German Diaries, 7 February 1937, Beckett International Foundation, University of Reading, quoted in Mark Nixon, *Samuel Beckett's German Diaries, 1936–37*, Continuum, London, 2011, p. 211.
72. Samuel Beckett, *Molloy*, ed. Shane Weller, Faber & Faber, London, 2010, p. 22.
73. Ibid., p. 140.
74. UoR MS 1227-7-12-1, fol. 01r. Quoted in James Little, *The Making of 'Not I / Pas Moi', 'That Time / Cette fois', and 'Footfalls / Pas'*, Bloomsbury, London, 2021, p. 161.
75. UoR MS 1227-7-12-6, fol. 01r.

76. Beckett, *The Collected Poems of Samuel Beckett*, p. 221.
77. Quoted in Dirk Van Hulle, 'The Manuscripts of Beckett's Late Poems', in James Brophy and William Davies (eds), *Samuel Beckett's Poetry*, Cambridge University Press, Cambridge, 2022, p. 227.
78. Quoted in Mark Nixon, '"The Remains of Trace": Intra- and Intertextual Transference in Beckett's mirlitonnades Manuscripts', *Journal of Beckett Studies*, vol. 16, no. 1–2, 2006, p. 118.
79. Samuel Beckett, *Endgame*, Faber & Faber, London, 2009, p. 6.
80. Beckett, *Molloy*, p. 22.
81. See Steve Nicholson, *The Censorship of British Drama 1900–1968*, Volume 3: *The Fifties,* University of Exeter Press, Exeter, 2011, p. 47.
82. Lord Chamberlain Play Collection at the British Library (MS-BL-LCP-1954-23).
83. For the full list, see Dirk Van Hulle and Pim Verhulst, *The Making of 'En attendant Godot / Waiting for Godot'*, Bloomsbury, London, 2017, pp. 59–64.
84. British Library, Lord Chamberlain Play collection CORR 1954/6597.
85. Samuel Beckett, *En attendant Godot / Waiting for Godot: A Digital Genetic Edition*, ed. Dirk Van Hulle, Pim Verhulst and Vincent Neyt, Beckett Digital Manuscript Project BDMP6, University Press Antwerp, Brussels, 2017, ETLC, fol. 09r.
86. Samuel Beckett, *Waiting for Godot*, Faber & Faber, London, 1956, p. 17.
87. Harry Ransom Center, Austin TX, Donal Albery papers; quoted in Dirk Van Hulle and Shane Weller, *The Making of 'Fin de partie / Endgame'*, Bloomsbury, London, 2018, p. 63.
88. Samuel Beckett, *The Letters of Samuel Beckett*, Volume 3: *1957–1965*, ed. George Craig, Martha Dow Fehsenfeld, Dan Gunn and Lois More Overbeck, Cambridge University Press, Cambridge, 2014, p. 16.
89. Ibid., p. 81.
90. Ibid., p. 83.
91. Quoted in Van Hulle and Weller, *Endgame*, p. 264.
92. David Leeming, *Stephen Spender: A Life in Modernism*, Duckworth, London, 1999, p. 37.
93. We owe a debt of gratitude to Clara Abbott, who made a digital edition of the changing dedications in Spender's *The Temple*.
94. Quoted in Samuel Hynes, 'Boys in Berlin', *The New Republic*, vol. 19, no. 5, 1988, p. 53.
95. Stephen Spender, *The Temple*, Faber & Faber, London, 1988, p. ix.
96. Stephen Spender, *Journals: 1939–1983*, ed. John Goldsmith, Faber & Faber, London, 1985, pp. 388–9.
97. Bodleian Library, MS. Spender 330, fol. 16r.
98. Raymonde Debray Genette, 'Flaubert's "A Simple Heart," or How to Make an Ending', in Jed Deppman, Daniel Ferrer and Michael Groden (eds), *Genetic Criticism*, University of Pennsylvania Press, Philadelphia PA, 2004, p. 70.
99. Niels Buch Leander, *The Sense of a Beginning: Theory of the Literary Opening*, Museum Tusculanum Press, Copenhagen, 2018, p. 46.
100. Ibid., p. 45.
101. Ibid., p. 46.
102. Debray Genette, '*Flaubert's* "A Simple Heart"', p. 72.
103. Raymond Chandler, *The Long Good-bye*, Penguin, London, 2010, p. 447.
104. Ibid., p. 448.
105. James Edward Austen-Leigh, *A Memoir of Jane Austen,* 2nd edn, Bentley, London, 1871, p. 125.
106. Jane Austen, *Persuasion*, Dent, Dutton, London, 1922, pp. 202–3.
107. Alan Bennett, *The Madness of George III*, Faber & Faber, London, 1995, p. ix.
108. Nicholas Hytner, *Balancing Acts: Behind the Scenes at the National Theatre*, Vintage, London, 2018, p. 118.

109. Bodleian MS. Bennett 146:334.
110. Bennett, *The Madness of George III*, p. xix.
111. Bodleian MS. Bennett 146:337.
112. Ibid.
113. Bodleian MS. Bennett 146:338.
114. Hytner, *Balancing Acts*, p. 118.
115. Bennett, *The Madness of George III*, p. xix.
116. Bodleian MS. Bennett 146:588.
117. Nicholas Hytner, 'Interview with Duncan Wu', in Duncan Wu (ed.), *Making Plays: Interviews with Contemporary British Dramatists and Directors*, Macmillan, Basingstoke, 2000, p. 109.
118. Bodleian MS. Bennett 147:1.
119. Bodleian MS. Bennett 147:90.
120. Bodleian MS. Bennett 147:91.
121. Bodleian MS. Bennett 147:359/360.
122. Bodleian MS. Bennett 148:523.
123. Hytner, *Balancing Acts*, pp. 119, 120.
124. Bennett, *The Madness of George III*, p. xi.
125. Ibid.
126. Hytner, 'Interview with Duncan Wu', p. 110.
127. Saint-John Perse, *Anabasis*, trans. T.S. Eliot, Faber & Faber, London, 1930, p. 32; emphasis added.
128. FSJP MS. Larbaud FSJP, fol. 4r; emphasis added.
129. Perse, *Anabasis*, p. 33; emphasis added.
130. Saint-John Perse, *Œuvres completes*, Collection 'Bibliothèque de la Pléiade', Gallimard, Paris, 1972, p. 98; emphasis added.
131. Bodleian MS. Don. c. 23/2, fol. 8r; emphasis added.
132. Valery Larbaud, 'Answers and explanations' (MS 11 fols), 1929, Fondation Saint-John Perse (FSJP), Aix-en-Provence. FSJP MS. Larbaud, fol. 4r; quoted in Patrick Hersant, 'La troisième main: réviser la traduction littéraire', in Esa Hartmann and Patrick Hersant (eds), *Au miroir de la traduction: Avant-texte, intratexte, paratexte*, Editions des archives contemporaines, Paris, 2019, pp. 45–70, esp. p. 48.
133. Perse, *Anabasis*, p. 33; emphasis added.
134. Eliot in Perse, *Anabasis*, p. 7
135. Ibid., pp. 7–8; emphasis added.
136. Perse, *Anabasis*, p. 18; emphasis added.
137. Ibid., p. 19; emphasis added.
138. Dirk Van Hulle, *Modern Manuscripts: The Extended Mind and Creative Undoing from Darwin to Beckett and Beyond*, Bloomsbury, London, 2014, p. 227.
139. Percy Bysshe Shelley, *The Bodleian Shelley Manuscripts*, Volume XI: *The Geneva Notebook*, transcribed and ed. Michael Erkelenz, Garland, New York and London, 1992, pp. 126–7; Bodleian MS. Shelley Adds. c.4, fol. 65r.
140. Bodleian MS. Abinger c.57, fols 73r–73v. Charles E. Robinson, 'Percy Shelley's Text(s) in Mary Wollstonecraft Shelley's Frankenstein', in Alan M. Weinberg and Timothy Webb (eds.), *The Neglected Shelley*, Routledge, London and New York, 2015, p. 126.
141. Bodleian MS. Abinger c.57, fol. 73v; emphasis added.
142. Bodleian MS. Auct. D. inf. 2.11, digital.bodleian.ox.ac.uk/objects/c070934c-79ca-426c-a115-aee7d810579e/surfaces/fd1bb77a-ddc5-4d0c-ab1a-4366f60c0cd6.
143. Bodleian MS. Eng. c. 7445/54. We owe a debt of gratitude to Chris Fletcher, who drew our attention to this material in the Bodleian, and who also traced a copy of the draft (dated 21 July 1982) of Larkin's poem to the University of Hull Library (Hull DPL 1/8/51).
144. Philip Larkin, *The Complete Poems*, rev. edn, ed. Archie Burnett, Faber & Faber, London, 2018, p. 323; annotation pp. 664–5.

145. The poem is included in *The Complete Poems*, edited with excellent annotations by Archie Burnett, Faber & Faber, London, 2014. The print format presents the poem '1982' in the section 'poems not published in the poet's lifetime' as a title and ten lines of text. The annotation at the back of the volume concisely gives as much information as possible, but for readers it remains hard to picture the visuality of the manuscript.
146. Tom Paulin, *Minotaur: Poetry in the Nation State*, Faber & Faber, London, 1993, p. 236.
147. Bodleian Library, Owen MSS OEF 207.
148. John Keats, 'Lines on Seeing a Lock of Milton's Hair', in *John Keats: The Major Works*, ed. Elizabeth Cook, Oxford University Press, Oxford, 1990.
149. Osbert Sitwell, 'Wilfred Owen', *The Atlantic,* August 1950, www.theatlantic.com/magazine/archive/1950/08/wilfred-owen/639514.
150. Susan J. Wolfson, 'Keats to Shelley: Load every rift', *The Keats Letters Project* (16 August 2020), keatslettersproject.com/correspondence/load-every-rift.
151. Wilfred Owen, *The Complete Poems and Fragments*, Volume II: *The Manuscripts of the Poems and the Fragments*, ed. Jon Stallworthy, Chatto & Windus, London, 1983, p. 293.
152. Matthew G. Kirschenbaum, *Mechanisms: New Media and the Forensic Imagination*, MIT Press, Cambridge MA, 2008; Kirschenbaum, 'The .txtual Condition: Digital Humanities, Born-Digital Archives, and the Future Literary', *Digital Humanities Quarterly*, vol. 7, no. 1, 2013, www.digitalhumanities.org/dhq/vol/7/1/000151/000151.html; Thorsten Ries, 'The Rationale of the Born-Digital *dossier génétique*: Digital Forensics and the Writing Process: With Examples from the Thomas Kling Archive', *Digital Scholarship in the Humanities*, vol. 33, no. 2, 2018, pp. 391–424.
153. Mick Imlah, *Selected Poems*, Faber & Faber, London, 2010, p. xii.
154. Mark Imlah, MS 12919/1, folder 2.
155. Both the 1937 and the 1961 films are available on YouTube: www.youtube.com/watch?v=_IJjyzvg1Uo (1937 version); www.youtube.com/watch?v=f5FHyn9F7eo (1961 version).
156. For a simulation of this imaginary genesis, see Dirk Van Hulle, 'Dynamic Facsimiles: Note on the Transcription of Born-Digital Works for Genetic Criticism', *Variants* 15–16, 2021, journals.openedition.org/variants/1450.
157. Craig M. Taylor, 'C M Taylor on "keystroke logging project" with British Library', *British Library English and Drama Blog*, 9 November 2018, blogs.bl.uk/english-and-drama/2018/11/c-m-taylor-on-keystroke-logging-project-with-british-library.html.
158. Ibid.
159. *Midst*, landing page, www.midst.press.
160. An emulated run of the poem based on a bit-level copy of an original diskette loaned by collector Allan Chasanoff William, played on a 1992-era Mac computer running the System 7 operating system, can be found at www.youtube.com/watch?v=41kZovcyHrU.
161. Ford encouraged Jean Rhys to develop and publish her early work. Katie Owen, 'Introduction' in Jean Rhys, *Quartet*, Penguin Classics, London, 2000, p. xiii.
162. Alice Oswald, 'The Art of Erosion', Inaugural Lecture held at the University of Oxford Exam Schools, 9 December 2019, University of Oxford Podcasts, podcasts.ox.ac.uk/art-erosion.
163. Samuel Beckett, letter to Axel Kaun, 9 July 1937, in *The Letters of Samuel Beckett*, vol. 1, p. 515.
164. Oswald, 'The Art of Erosion'.

FURTHER READING

Bryant, John, *The Fluid Text: A Theory of Revision and Editing for Book and Screen*, University of Michigan Press, Ann Arbor MI, 2002.

Chartier, Roger, *Inscription and Erasure*, trans. Arthur Goldhammer, University of Pennsylvania Press, Philadelphia PA, 2007.

Deppman, Jed, Daniel Ferrer and Michael Groden (eds), *Genetic Criticism: Texts and Avant-textes*, University of Pennsylvania Press, Philadelphia PA, 2004.

Ferrer, Daniel, 'Production, Invention and Reproduction: Genetic Criticism vs. Textual Criticism', in Neil Fraistat and Elizabeth Bergmann Loizeaux (eds), *Reimagining Textuality: Textual Studies in the Late Age of Print*, Wisconsin University Press, Madison WI, 2002.

Ferrer, Daniel, *Logiques du brouillon: Modèles pour une critique génétique*, Seuil, Paris, 2011.

Fordham, Finn, *I Do I Undo I Redo: The Textual Genesis of Modernist Selves*, Oxford University Press, Oxford, 2010.

Fraistat, Neil, and Julia Flanders (eds), *The Cambridge Companion to Textual Scholarship*, Cambridge University Press, Cambridge, 2013.

Gabler, Hans Walter, *Text Genetics in Literary Modernism and Other Essays*, Open Book, Cambridge, 2018.

Groenland, Tim, *The Art of Editing: Raymond Carver and David Foster Wallace*, Bloomsbury Academic, New York, 2019.

Kirschenbaum, Matthew G., *Mechanisms: New Media and the Forensic Imagination*, MIT Press, Cambridge MA, 2008.

Kirschenbaum, Matthew G., 'The .txtual Condition: Digital Humanities, Born-Digital Archives, and the Future Literary', *Digital Humanities Quarterly*, vol. 7, no. 1, 2013, www.digitalhumanities.org/dhq/vol/7/1/000151/000151.html.

Knowlson, James, *Damned to Fame: The Life of Samuel Beckett*, Bloomsbury, London, 1996.

Larkin, Philip, 'A Neglected Responsibility: Contemporary Literary Manuscripts', in *Required Reading: Miscellaneous Pieces, 1955–1982*, Faber & Faber, London, 1983, pp. 98–108.

Shillingsburg, Peter, *From Gutenberg to Google: Electronic Representations of Literary Texts*, Cambridge University Press, Cambridge, 2006.

Smith, Carrie, and Lisa Stead (eds), *The Boundaries of the Literary Archive: Reclamation and Representation*, Ashgate, Farnham, 2013.

Sullivan, Hannah, *The Work of Revision*, Harvard University Press, Cambridge MA, 2013.

Sutherland, Katheryn, *Why Modern Manuscripts Matter*, Oxford University Press, Oxford, 2022.

Van Hulle, Dirk, *Modern Manuscripts: The Extended Mind and Creative Undoing from Darwin to Beckett and Beyond*, Bloomsbury, London, 2014.

Van Hulle, Dirk, *Genetic Criticism: Tracing Creativity in Literature*, Oxford University Press, Oxford, 2022.

PICTURE & TEXT CREDITS

FIGS 4, 5, 12, 13, 43, 45, 46, 47, 48 Courtesy of the Beckett International Foundation, The University of Reading; © The Estate of Samuel Beckett.
FIGS 39, 40, 41, 42 Courtesy of Special Collections, The University of Reading; © The Estate of Samuel Beckett.
FIG. 7 Reproduced with the permission of the Estate of W.H. Auden.
FIG. 14 Reproduced with permission of Johnson & Alcock Ltd.
FIG. 15 © The Tolkien Estate Limited 1976, 1979.
FIGS 24, 25, 60 and 61 Copyright © The Estate of Raymond Chandler. Reproduced by permission of the Estate c/o Rogers, Coleridge & White Ltd., 20 Powis Mews, London W11 1JN.
FIGS 26–29 Reproduced with permission of the Estate of Ivor Treby.
FIG. 33 Reproduced with permission of Laura Morris Literary Agency on behalf of the Pym Estate.
FIGS 34 & 38 Reproduced by kind permission of Philip Pullman.
FIG. 35 By permission of the Estate of W.B. Yeats.
FIG. 37 copyright © Bruce Chatwin Estate.
FIG. 44 Burns Library, Boston College, Beckett collection/© The Estate of Samuel Beckett.
FIG. 49 British Library, London/Bridgeman Images/© The Estate of Samuel Beckett.
FIGS 50–52 Reproduced with permission of Curtis Brown Group Ltd, London on behalf of the Beneficiaries of The Estate of Stephen Spender. Copyright © Stephen Spender.
FIGS 53–58 © The John le Carré Literary Estate, reproduced with permission.
FIGS 59, 63–65 Reproduced with permission of United Agents on behalf of Alan Bennett.
FIGS 66–67 Manuscript of 'Anabasis' by T.S. Eliot reproduced by permission of Faber and Faber Ltd.
FIG. 68 Courtesy of Visual Editions.
FIG. 75 and p. 157 Excerpt from '1982' from *The Complete Poems of Philip Larkin* by Philip Larkin, edited by Archie Burnett. Copyright © 2012 by The Estate of Philip Larkin. Reprinted by permission of Farrar, Straus and Giroux. All Rights Reserved. Also by permission of the Society of Authors and Faber and Faber Ltd.
FIGS 77–78 By permission of the Trustees of the Wilfred Owen Estate.
FIG. 79 By permission of the Trustees of the Estate of Mick Imlah.
FIGS 82–84 By permission of Midst Press www.midst.press.
FIG. 85 By permission of Alice Oswald.

Quotations on pp. 104–7 from the Lord Chamberlain's papers held at the British Library reproduced under the Open Government Licence.

INDEX

References to images are in **bold** type